Old Ystrad Mynach

including

Hengoed, Cefn Hengoed and Maesycwmmer

in Photographs

by Maldwyn Griffiths and Richard Herold

Foreword by
Allan Rogers, B.Sc. F.R.G.S.
Former M.P. for Rhondda

Volume 1

Old Bakehouse Publications

Abertillery

First published in October 2001

ISBN 1 874538 39 5

Published in the U.K. by
Old Bakehouse Publications
Church Street,
Abertillery, Gwent NP13 1EA
Telephone: 01495 212600 Fax: 01495 216222
www.mediamaster.co.uk/oldbakebooks

Made and printed in the UK
by J.R. Davies (Printers) Ltd.

Foreword

by

Allan Rogers
Former Member of Parliament for Rhondda

As a native of the area I am delighted to have been asked to write this foreword.

Gelligaer, Hengoed, Ystrad Mynach and Maesycwmmer are all steeped in history. The iron-age fort, Roman fort and Villa, Norman Church and Ty Cwrdd (Hengoed Old Welsh Chapel) provide us with evidence of long and sustained settlement reaching back thousands of years.

The last century saw the sinking of Penallta Colliery, the trigger for inward migration that was to lead to the growth of Ystrad Mynach and the creation of the villages of Penybryn, Cefn Hengoed, Tiryberth, Glyngaer and Cascade.

These communities have been added to from the late 1940s, culminating in recent years with substantial housing development around and between existing villages. This book by Maldwyn Griffiths and Richard Herold records visually this great historical record and I am privileged to be associated with its publication.

Allan Rogers

Allan Rogers

Contents

Introduction

The inspiration for this book was the result of a reunion that was held in 1999 of people from Hengoed and the surrounding villages. A further such reunion was organized in March 2001 which proved to be as equally successful as its predecessor with more than 300 attending, the proceeds of which were passed to Ystrad Mynach Boys and Girls Club. These events have proved beyond doubt that the community spirit in the district is alive and well and at that time, opinions were expressed that a book about the area and its population was long overdue - other parts of the valley already having received such attention.

The sheer number of names recorded on the final page well-illustrate the enthusiasm that we have received for this publication. To each and every one who has provided photographs, information and valuable time, we extend our sincere thanks; if by pure accident we have omitted anyone, would they please accept our humble apologies. Amidst the other pages will be found a number of stories of local people who will be remembered as characters in every sense of the word, too many in fact to include in one volume which leaves the door wide open for a sequel in due course.

The district is rich with academic, sporting and entertainment achievers. To name just one for instance there is entertainments manager Willy Hamilton of Ystrad Mynach, responsible for bringing top pop groups of the 1960s to the town and who was just a whisker away from signing up the Beatles for a performance at the Institute Hall, only to be beaten at the last minute by the town of Abergavenny, their larger premises winning the day. The opening chapter deals with the towns and villages and the way they appeared in times past and whilst some of the scenes will seem familiar to a number of readers, there will be many who might be a little bewildered by the transformation that has now taken place. Hopefully therefore, this publication will contain something to please everyone.

Our final thanks must go to our wives and families, who have been more than tolerant during the time it has taken to produce this book and their understanding and encouragement is much appreciated.

Maldwyn Griffiths   *Richard Head*

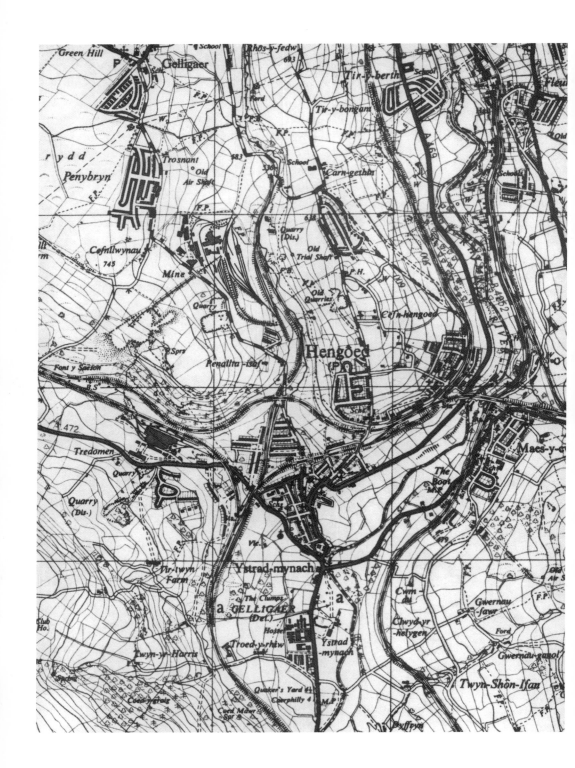

CHAPTER 1

Ystrad Mynach

1. This view looking north towards the Beech Tree Hotel Square on Bedwlyn Road is from days when the area was quite a busy little shopping centre. Pedestrians are pictured outside Fine's outfitters and shoe shop with Bracchi's Café next on the left, Giovanni Brachi seen standing in the doorway. The advertisement on the hotel offers accommodation to motorists together with petrol, repairs and service. The petrol on offer may well have been sold from a hand pump or in one-gallon cans at the time, the price a *'hard to believe'* 4 pence a gallon compared to today's £4 and a pair of girls' shoes might have set one back for a mere 25p. Two other important and well-frequented buildings and places of entertainment on the square and opposite the hotel, are the Palace Cinema and the Lucania Billiard Hall.

2. This scene of a *'young'* Ystrad Mynach is viewed from the Graig Hengoed and was photographed before Bedwlyn Street, Dilwyn Avenue or The Walk had been constructed. The Beech Tree hotel is also to be seen with its large car park on the left. Another familiar sight from the past is the steam-hauled train making its way up towards the Rhymney Valley with a load of empty Powell Duffryn Company trucks ready to be filled with coal from their local colliery at Bargoed. A rare sight of the mountain landscape is also available prior to the coal waste of Llanbradach.

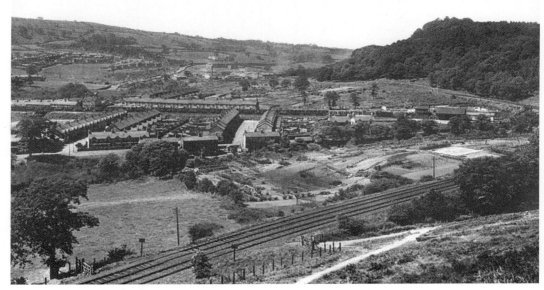

3. A general view of the northern area of Ystrad Mynach from the late 1930s that looks towards the outcrop of rocks towering above Tredomen Engineering Works and Bryn Mynach. The Vale of Neath railway line winds its way past open fields and allotments in the foreground and past the rocks in the distance.

4. An exceptional view of Commercial Street taken from the Pierhead which is likely to be from the early 1920s judging by the presence of just two motor cars on the left. Distantly may be seen the Snooker and Billiard Institute with Dorothy's Café and the London House building on the right. Beneath the road in the foreground runs the Cylla Brook which then finds it way out at the back of the building on the left and in much earlier times a woollen mill once existed near Rose Cottage, half way down Commercial Street.

5. More *'early days'* in the centre of the town and the scene shows Lower Bedwlyn Road looking towards London House with Olivers shoe shop and Jones Arcade on the right which was built in 1912. On the opposite side of the road is the Imperial store, the shop belonging to D.J. Evans with familiar hand carts parked on both sides of the road. At one time, before these buildings and Commercial Street were erected, a steep incline was to be found here all the way down to the Royal Oak Hotel, providing a popular ride for local children and their homemade carts.

6. A peaceful looking scene at Bedwlyn Road with just two modes of transport in sight, namely a horse and cart and a vintage car parked outside the hotel. The area on the left with the Beech and neighbouring cottages was at one time mysteriously known as *'The Shant'*.

7. Another view of the square Bedwlyn Road, this time looking downwards in about 1920 with just one motor car outside the hotel and a water trough for the still much used horsedrawn traffic; according to the hotel's sign, a certain *'M. Price'* was the Beech Tree's proprietor at the time. There were a number of shops on the left here such as Cash for hardware, with a tin bath hanging up on display and other businesses close by included Pegler's (well known grocery shops in the Welsh valleys), Watkins the drapers and Morgan the chemist. Further along straight ahead was Kirby the popular butchers.

8. A relatively quiet scene in Bedwlyn Street during the 1930s with some deliveries being made to local shops. The lady and gentleman on the left are stood outside Paris House, a former exclusive shop for ladies wear and Mrs. Peggy Holder recalls visiting this shop with her mother regularly during this period. One of the owners of Paris House was a Miss Maria Smith from Maesycwmmer and Mrs. Holder remembers her having a distinctive hairstyle for the time called *'Wireless Style'* - plaits curled around the ears.

9. From the 1950s comes this scene which was photographed from over the bridge looking to the once thriving garage belonging to Glam Mon Motors, complete with fuel pumps on the forecourt; standing close by is another building to be remembered - the old school house.

11

10. This must be regarded as an exceptional photograph taken at Ystrad Mynach railway station and the stationmaster's house in the very early part of the twentieth century. The horse and cart belonged to the Rhymney Railway Company who owned the lines at this time, the cart being used for the distribution of parcels and merchandise.

11. Another picture from about the same period as the previous photograph, once again illustrating the importance of horse power. The scene is at Bedwlyn Road with Mr. William Ernest Kirby in the doorway of his butcher's shop adjacent to Ernest James and his ironmongery store. On the opposite side of the road, on the corner stands Fines the outfitters and more distantly is Bedwlyn House which is nowadays the Workingmen's Club. The two shops on the left still trade in the same professions as Walters the butchers and Emlyn Lloyd the ironmongers.

12. A 1960s view of Caerphilly Road, the large white building being the Ystrad Mynach clinic. Further afield is Hengoed with the Institute at the top which has long been demolished. Another familiar sight from the past can be seen in the distance - a West Mon double-decker bus on its way to Caerphilly from Blackwood.

13. The *'Bevin Huts'* which were a familiar sight in Ystrad Mynach some years ago. These were government sponsored buildings that were intended as temporary accommodation for workers who came to the area when colliery jobs were plentiful. They were also used to house a variety of displaced persons from the continent who sought refuge in this country following the Second World War. This site is now occupied by the hospital.

14. The impressive old School House as it appeared in about 1918, a building that possessed a most ornate entrance archway. The gas lamp standard rests in the centre of the crossroads from Caerphilly, Maesycwmmer and Ystrad Mynach with just one or two citizens posing for the camera. The cottage on the left was subsequently demolished to make way for some necessary road improvements, as time went by.

15. Royal Oak Square with the Royal Oak in the background as pictured from the location of the old School House. There is no traffic to be seen at the time but today it will be better recognised as a busy junction from where transport makes its way to the town centre. The small white cottage to the right of the Royal Oak has since been demolished, the ground now forming part of the car park.

16. A quiet and traffic-free Church Street, Ystrad Mynach as it would have looked in 1920. The main sign of activity is a steam train in the distance which is making its way towards Cardiff.

17. A not too busy-looking Pengam Road around the late 1920s early 1930s. The most imposing building to be seen on the right is Ystrad Mynach Police Station, it having opened for service in 1925.

18. This particular photograph is almost a hundred years old and shows Pontargylla with a group of locals posing for a visiting cameraman. Two, who have been positively identified are Will and Jane Davies (known as Ginny), seen standing in the doorway of their cottage.

19. This view from the 1960s has been photographed from almost the same position as the early one of Pontargylla seen above. It can be seen that Ystrad Mynach has by now developed into a sizeable shopping town with the Pierhead as a focal point. Originally this building belonged to the Ystrad Mynach branch of the Treharris Workmen's Co-operative Society, and some more mature readers will recall Co-op Stores in most valley towns with their system of paying a cash dividend (or divi) to their customers. Mr. Moore of Gelligroes is seen with his motorcycle outside the Co-op with Mr. Cliff Coles's car parked outside his office.

20. Penallta Road as it was during the 1950s with a few shoppers biding their time, and a car and van parked in opposite directions reminding us that the volume of traffic in those days allowed for a two-way system along the road. John and Lena's Café is one of the few establishments still in business with Lena still happy to serve her customers.

21. What was once a most popular and well-attended event was the annual Whitsun *'turnout'*, organized collectively by the various religious bodies in the town. The scene is set here in the square with Mr. Stevens conducting the Penallta Band together with the mixed chapels and church lads brigade led by Con Bowen. Vicar Williams with the white hat stands in the front and others in the crowd have been identified as Evan Richards, Austin Henry and Jack Hopkins. Following the performance, the big treats to be enjoyed by all would be the tea parties held in the local chapels and churches and then on to the Trinity Fields for the Whitsun games.

22. There are some elegantly dressed gentlemen posing for the camera here in about 1920 who are stood on the new bridge. Spanning the Rhymney river, it formed the links with Caerphilly Road and Nelson Road to Maesycwmmer.

23. The concluding photograph in this first chapter is of the mansion house known as Ystrad Fawr or Ystrad House as it was once called. This magnificent house was formerly home to two families who played an important part in the development of the Ystrad Mynach area, namely the Thomas's and the Lindsay's. They were both well known for their supportiveness of the church and charitable work; the grounds of this fine house were often used for grand tea parties and sporting events during the summer months.

CHAPTER 2

Hengoed

24. The first picture in this second chapter is of Lower Kings Hill and looks towards the viaduct. There are a number of shops on the left that have long been closed and converted into flats and the rooms above were formerly occupied by the Billiard Hall and a small restaurant. Also to be noticed are two gentlemen sitting on the fence beneath the viaduct, this at one time being a popular meeting point on Sunday mornings for regulars awaiting opening time at the Junction Public House.

25. The period is the 1920s and the pedestrians posing for the cameraman include a young mother holding a child and a lad with his push bike. All of this is taking place outside William and Harriet Evans's hardware shop in Brynavon Terrace Hengoed. This was a busy part of the town with a collection of shops available such as a chemist, newsagent, butchers, bakers and clothing. The building on the far right has been trading as a hairdresser's for more than fifty years and now known as the Edwardian Studios.

26. Park Road as it appeared some ninety years ago which at the time ran alongside the Neath to Pontypool railway line. This part of Hengoed was occupied mainly by professional persons and had a sense of opulence about it, quite a number of the residents being employers of servants and housemaids.

27. An aerial view of Hengoed and Maesycwmmer taken some time after the completion of the New Road from Ystrad Mynach to Gilfach in 1920. Many former landmarks can be seen such as the railway sidings at Hengoed whilst on the right of the picture are the old main road, Commercial Street and the Brecon and Merthyr railway lines to Newport.

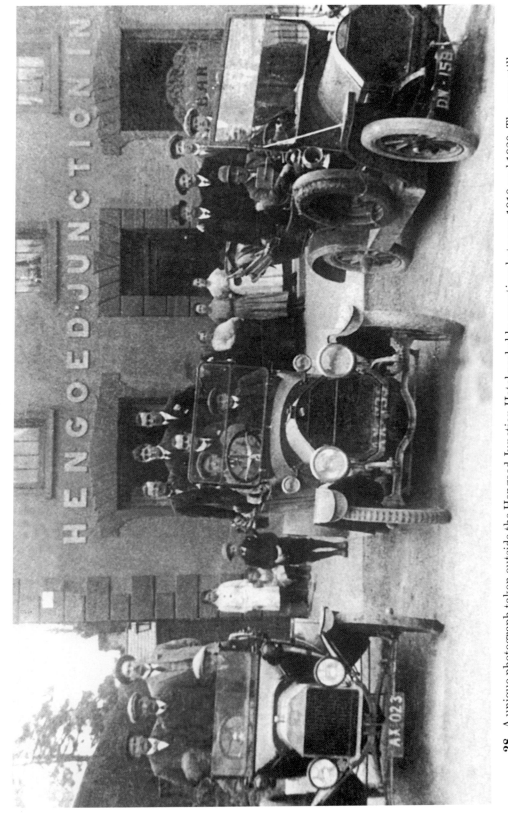

28. A unique photograph taken outside the Hengoed Junction Hotel probably sometime between 1910 and 1920. The cars still have solid rubber tyres and some early AX (Monmouthshire) registration plates. Some local gentlemen in the picture include brothers Trevor and Norman Whatley and Mr. Wayman.

29. Possibly from as early as the year 1875 comes this picture showing such features as the Junction Hotel with customers sitting outside on the windowsill with the landlady stood in the doorway. The cottages below on Kings Hill were later converted into a number of shops and to the rear of these cottages can be seen the Glamorgan House in Raglan Road complete with servants working in an impressive vegetable garden.

30. This is a similar view taken of lower Hengoed some thirty years later. It may be seen that the Glamorgan House has now had a few improvements such as an entry porch, walls rendered white and the vegetable garden has been converted to a fine green plot with members of the household stood on the lawn. High above can be seen the Hengoed County Girls School and the Hengoed Wagon Works.

31. This full sized photograph taken in around 1902-03 of Hengoed, north of the viaduct deserves some careful study as this is how the area would have looked prior to the development of Raglan Road. The vegetable garden was a familiar sight and can be clearly seen at Club Row.

32. Raglan Road during days when the Picturedrome stood as a modern and fascinating place of early silent films and the children seen here are probably waiting to be entertained by the likes of Charlie Chaplin and The Keystone Cops. Mr. Arthur Roberts recalls himself and his brother each paying two pence admission and a halfpenny for sweets (a total of 1p in today's currency) in the year 1917. Underneath and to the rear of the cinema was a small dance hall, for some reason known as *'The Chicken Run'*. To the left stands the postal sorting office with a fish shop, cobblers and barbers shop further down the road. Jack (Piano) Davies used to play the piano to the silent movies at this time.

33. This picture was taken from the footbridge access to the High Level station at Hengoed and shows the goods yard entrance with Park Road in the background in 1920. Hengoed High Level was once a junction for two railway companies, those of the Rhymney Railway Company and Taff Vale and would have been the first stop for passenger trains which had crossed the viaduct from the direction of Pontypool.

34. A glance over the roof tops surrounding the stationmaster's house and the Junction Hotel. The advertisement on the pine end of the hotel tells us that its ales were supplied at the time by an old established brewer and wine merchant of Merthyr Tydfil, Giles and Harrap; landlord and landlady for many years were Roland and Sarah Ann Edwards.

35./36. Two early views of Hengoed Council Offices on Park Road. Built in 1897 at a cost of almost £1300 the building was home to the offices of the Gelligaer and Rhigos Rural District Council. Prior to the Local Government Act of 1894, matters for the Gelligaer district were governed by a Parish Vestry Meeting under the auspices of the local rector, it being responsible for such bodies as surveyors of the highways and parish constables. By 1908 the population of Gelligaer far exceeded that of Rhigos and the inhabitants demanded a greater say in the running of their affairs and consequently the Urban District of Gelligaer was formed during that year. At the time of these photographs the Council Chairman was Mr. Edward Richards of Ystrad Mynach. Unfortunately the fine Victorian building pictured here was destroyed by fire in 1968.

37. Hengoed's old fire station, another fine architectural example from the late nineteenth century which used to stand in Park Road next to the Council Offices. In the early years the local fire service would have been a pure voluntary organisation and was formed in about 1905 with headquarters in Gilfach; the fire appliance at the time was comprised of a hand hauled cart, complete with a tank of water and manually operated pump. The building seen here was saved, dismantled and reconstructed at Ystrad Fawr Grounds, Ystrad Mynach.

38. Another look at Park Road from days when it was not necessary to have a particularly hard road surface and street lighting was confined to a solitary gas standard which young children take to leaning on in about 1916.

39. A superb view of the viaduct showing all of its sixteen arches and the gentle curve sweeping across to Maesycwmmer. As an excellent example of Victorian railway architecture, it stands at 130 feet high and 298 yards long and was opened for traffic in 1857. Once the viaduct was completed for the Newport, Abergavenny and Hereford Railway Company, it provided a much needed extension of the lines from Pontypool, Crumlin and onto Quakers Yard. Another line which ran beneath the viaduct as seen on page 35, was the property of the Brecon and Merthyr Railway, the route following the Rhymney Valley.

40. The old approach to Hengoed High Level with the station office at the top of the rise during the 1950s. The station was opened for traffic in about 1858 following completion of the viaduct crossing the Rhymney river. The excellent facilities of the railway companies are shown here with the view of the waiting room on high and low level platforms.

41. The area of Hengoed which has been photographed from the viaduct in about 1920. The building of the new road is in progress with major alterations to Hills Terrace in the foreground. The cottages at the bottom of the hill have been demolished. This part of Hengoed has grown considerably from the photograph on page 26 with the building of Raglan Road, Alexandra Road, Bryn Terrace, Beechfield Avenue and James Terrace at the top left.

42. The lower part of King's Hill during the 1970s, a period when the decline of the corner shops was taking effect. These businesses changed hands several times while Ivor Teconi the grocer was the longest serving proprietor. The Junction and Stationmaster's house are other prominent buildings to be noted.

43./44. This farm, situated in Park Road next to the Council Offices and adjacent to Hengoed Station was considered by some to have been a piece of local architecture well worth preserving. Alas this old-style farmhouse was in dire need of some essential improvements and consequently could not be sufficiently preserved to qualify as a full listed building and survive the passing of time. In the lower picture Mr. Dan Herbert is seen in the farmhouse yard surrounded by Betty, Phyllis, Gwladys, Margaret, Elizabeth, Megan, Jean Griffiths and babies Eileen and Jane.

CHAPTER 3

Maesycwmmer

45. A view through the arches of the Hengoed - Maesycwmmer viaduct with the railway track curving its way round shortly after leaving Maesycwmmer station. A superb example of 19th-century railway architecture, it comprises of sixteen arches and seen here is the eastern arch that is skewed to allow it to span the Brecon and Merthyr railway lines running below at quite an angle. The large building on the right is the gable end of the Butcher's Arms with Victoria Lane winding its way alongside the railway track to the left and through the archway All Saints Church and Gelihaf are in view.

46. A photograph taken from the viaduct in the early 1960s looks down onto the square in Maesycwmmer. Some prominent buildings in the foreground include the Butcher's Arms and the Angel with their outbuildings which were originally used as stables and in more modern times as garages and storerooms. The remains of the old bakehouse may be seen next to the top of the double-decker bus and on the right of the picture stands the railway station, now boarded up.

47. Summerfield Lane and Maesycwmmer Church are featured in this scene from the viaduct as is Summerfield Hall and Gellihaf further along. The old Brecon and Merthyr railway line which used to run alongside Victoria Road has been removed, the church has since been demolished and the ground has now been completely rebuilt on. Arthur Roberts of Hengoed and Dolly May Powell had the honour to be the first couple to get wed in this church in 1931.

48. A fine view of Maesycwmmer which was taken from Hengoed High Level Station. The station and the original square to the left of the picture shows just how the area looked before the new road was built. The building standing prominently below Tabor Chapel was at the time the Democrat Club which was burnt down in about 1951. The little cottage in the centre was once the home of Mr. Reg Hurcombe and also to be noticed is a small orchard, next to what is now Hill View Guest House.

49. The square Maesycwmmer, and stood in the centre having his photograph taken is the local stationmaster. The date is approximately 1906 and if so, then the stationmaster would have been Mr. William Davies. Behind the gentleman are Station Cottages, Thomas Street and to the right is the Angel Inn with the Butcher's Arms just behind.

50. A view of the old main road, Commercial Street in Maesycwmmer taken in 1937. The road from the square to Ystrad Mynach had a series of bends and the road improvements of the late 1960s were a major benefit to motorists travelling through the village. Sadly the cottage on the left and the old style telegraph pole that was so common no longer exist. The old Democratic Club can be seen at the top of the road.

51. The open-air swimming baths pictured during construction. This was a local amenity built by the Maesycwmmer Welfare Association on land donated by Miss Ann Richards of Gwerna Farm, with necessary building materials being purchased through many fund-raising events and welcomed contributions from the public. There was an enthusiastic labour force available too, made up of local miners and tradesmen, all suitably refreshed by a group of lady helpers. Some of the Association members included such names as Horace Curtis, W.A. Davies, Abraham Moore, Morgan James (the woollen mill) and Richard Williams.

52. From about 1910 comes this view looking down onto The Mill and Maesycwmmer House, the name having been given to the village as it then was. This original postcard was sent by someone employed at the local post office in Raglan Road who has marked an 'X', as seen through an archway, informing us of the office's whereabouts.

53. An interesting picture from the platform of Maesycwmmer station with trains travelling in all directions. On the viaduct, goods trains are passing on the Pontypool to Neath line, whilst below, a steam train pulls in from the direction of Aberbargoed. During the early years of the railway system here, there was an amount of confusion for passengers over station names, due to differing railway companies operating the services in the district. Hengoed High Level was called Hengoed and Maesycwmmer, whilst Maesycwmmer station seen here, was called Maesycwmmer and Hengoed. The competiveness of the companies was finally settled in 1923 when the Great Western Railway took command. As local travellers will know, the only station left is the former Hengoed Low Level, known these days simply as 'Hengoed'.

54. Mr. Morgan James who was at one time the owner of the woollen mill is seen standing in the doorway of the mill building accompanied by his pet dog.

55. Another gentleman with long-standing connections with the mill - Mr. Harry Holder. He started work here in 1930 as the chauffeur, then working his way through several positions to become the chief wool grader. Harry finally retired after an astounding 47 years service.

56. The mill and outbuildings belonging to Morgan James's woollen mill. The premises were built in the middle of the eighteenth century as a corn mill before being converted to wool manufacturing, a place where the *'Welsh viaduct shirt'* could be found.

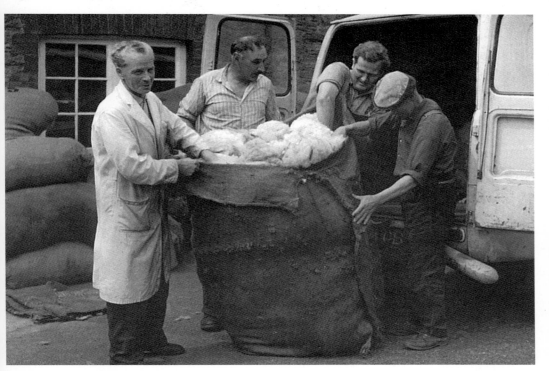

57. The grading of wool is a most important step in the manufacture of quality wool and Harry Holder, Gethin Hughes, Ross Williams and Jackie the driver are seen here inspecting a consignment which has just been delivered to the mill. Mr. Holder's duties included visiting numerous farms in the area to examine and scrutinize their product before purchasing.

58. A truck belonging to J. Boulton Transport of Merthyr Tydfil appears to be extremely well stacked with a delivery of wool, as the driver and his assistant prepare to unload their cargo at the mill during the 1960s.

59. This is quite a rare photograph taken of members of the local hunt who have stopped off at the Railway Junction Inn for a rest and liquid refreshment. This ale house is no longer standing but it once stood at the lower end of a block of houses in Main Road. It is possible that it is the Tredegar Farmers Hunt and that the gentleman in the the distinctive tall hat is Billy Thomas of Gwerna Farm.

60. Taken from the top end of Maesycwmmer in the late 1950s by engineers from the Highways Dept. whilst doing a levelling survey for future road improvements. This was vital to the increasing volume of traffic on this bend and bridge over the railway line to Pontypool. On the left Mr. E. Davies had a garage workshop and spares department for cars and motorbikes. Zoar Cottages and Old Zoar Calvinistic Methodist Chapel, erected in 1863, are prominently seen in the centre of the photograph.

CHAPTER 4

Industry, Trade and Transport

61. Penallta Colliery, which was a provider of jobs in the district for eighty years. The pit was opened in 1906 and owned by the Powell Duffryn Steam Coal Company, one of the largest such companies in South Wales, at their peak in the 1930s owning some 75 collieries. The picture shown above is of No.2 upcast shaft during the 1940s.

62. A general view of Penallta Colliery taken from the Graig Hengoed. In the distance may be seen Penybryn Terrace, known as the forty houses, these being the first to be built in Penybryn. Numbers 1 and 2 shafts stand prominently in the centre of the picture with the conveyor belt leading to the washery and there are hundreds of Powell Duffryn trucks waiting to be loaded on the Cylla branch of GWR's extension from Ystrad Mynach.

63. The Number 1 shaft entrance is seen again in the foreground as pictured from the canteen area and the large building to the left is the power house accommodating all the necessary machinery. Clear warning signs are visible asking colliery workers to search themselves for anything inflammable for obvious reasons before going underground.

64./65. Two views of the all-important engineering works at Tredomen as they looked in 1923. Tredomen served the National Coal Board, as it was once known, producing a wide variety of components as required in the mining industry. In the lower picture, the busy interior is seen with belt-driven lathes used for machining countless numbers of wheels for the trucks and trams from original castings made in the foundry; note also the large heavy duty overhead crane that was used to move components around the workshop.

66. The brothers Giovanni and Luigi Bracchi are seen standing proudly outside their café in Bedwlyn Road Ystrad Mynach during the 1920s. This was an Italian café of real Art Deco design and charm and a virtual social centre of the town where youngsters would congregate to enjoy the cappuccino coffee, dispensed from magnificent silver-coloured machines, hot sarsaparilla drinks (once unique to latter day cafés), pies and pasties that were heated by steam and of course, the famous Bracchi ice cream.

67. Pictured on Penallta Road Ystrad Mynach is Steve, in charge of Bess a faithful horse selling Bracchi ices with a few local miners standing in Glen View probably after a hard day's labour at Penallta Colliery and in need of a hot bath, there being no pit-baths provided for the workers in those days.

68. A familiar face from some years ago is that of Mr. Billy Hughes and his ice cream delivery service. He sits here on his new acquisition, a motor bike and sidecar, a vast improvement on his previous method of transport; this was a push bike and cart which Billy could be seen pedalling around the district with that well-known slogan *'Stop Me and Buy One'*.

69. Billy Hughes (more affectionately known as *'Billy The Chips'* and his wife Iris May started selling fish and chips from a coal-fired cart drawn by a horse named *'Dolly'* during the 1930s. Some time later they saw an opening for making and selling ice cream, crisps and sweets all being produced in a little tin sheet building at 23 Oak Terrace, Fleur De Lys, this by the 1960s developing into a family business with their son and daughter Howard and Lynn aided by around fifteen staff. The business flourished and at its height had some

fifteen chip and ice cream vans at its disposal and locals will also remember Hughes's Crisps a popular delicacy in the valley's pubs and shops. Even today the family name continues with Lynn and her daughter often seen with their vans catering for local appetites.

70. On the right is Evans's Store in Hengoed Crescent, Cefn Hengoed and next door on the left is Mr. Gibbons's butcher's shop where ox beef and wether mutton are offered for discerning meat lovers. Not seen much these days, if at all, wether mutton was the name given specifically to the meat of a male castrated sheep!

71. Evans's Stores in Brynavon Terrace Hengoed in about 1920 and in view are Jack Oliver, William and Harriett Evans, Tommy Rawlings, Doris Gent, Doris Powell and a young Gwladys Evans. The Evans's had two horses for their delivery services namely Dolly and Prince and in this picture Dolly is seen with her cart.

72. Employees from the former Star Shop in Lower Bedwlyn Road which some readers may remember. This shop was situated just up from the Pierhead Arcade and the window display claims a variety of *'cheaper cake'* to be on sale.

73. The period is about 1920 with Mr. Richard Edwards of Cwmdu Farm having come to collect his daily papers from Mrs. Olive Gertrude at Webbs tobacco and newspaper shop Ystrad Mynach. Also in the picture are a young Norman Webb and a shop assistant. Mr. Alan Webb a surviving grandson of the original owners, recalls the business changing hands several times over the years such as Mrs. Spiller and Mrs. Howell of Church Street who made her own clothes on the premises.

74. A young Trevor Everson with wife Margaret and daughter Kim are about to partake of an ice cream in Lansbury Avenue during the 1950s. Trevor, fifty years on, is the proud owner of Everson sports and Trophies of Ystrad Mynach, a business he built up to be one of the largest such retailers in the country. A keen footballer in his younger days, he now prefers the gentler game of bowls which has produced many successes such as Rhymney Valley open pairs championship in 1994, Welsh over 60s pairs semi finalist in 1999 and runners up in 2000 to name but a few.

75. Three generations of the Everson family and assistants amidst a vast display of trophies, many of which have found their way into cabinets and onto shelves in homes throughout Great Britain. Seen here are Trevor, Gareth and Lucy Everson with Ricky Williams and Kelly Tudor.

76. The shop assistants belonging to Ruther's grocery store some years ago and unfortunately the authors have not been able to trace any names on this occasion. However the shop itself might be recalled by some former customers when it used to stand next to Barclays Bank and Jones the florist.

77. This time it's the turn of staff belonging to Pegler's the grocers to be photographed in 1913. Like Ruther's, Pegler's shops were to be found in quite a few Welsh valley towns until about the mid 1960s when places like the old corner shop were swamped by the arrival of supermarkets. The branch of Pegler's seen here was opposite the Beech Tree hotel, adjacent to the cinema and below the Lucania billiard hall.

78./79. Two pictures which illustrate that the ancient skills of the blacksmith are not dead and buried. Above, Mr. John West is seen beside his forge at Lower Ystrad Mynach having taken over the business in 1972 after leaving Gwynns Garage where he worked as a panel beater - a trade that might well have been helpful in joining the blacksmith's profession. The lower photograph shows the range of implements required in such a job, the key tool being the anvil in the foreground.

80. John West is seen again at work in his Ystrad Mynach forge, amidst a large quantity of horseshoes he has just produced. Apart from the traditional skills of a farrier, he has also worked for CADW on a number of churches and castles throughout Wales. Amongst his most noted work is the involvement in the making of the gates and railings for Kensington Palace, traditional gates for St. Brides Major in the Vale of Glamorgan and some more recent work in producing the gates and railings for Siloh Church in Oakfield Street Ystrad.

Dear blacksmith

S. LAMBIRTH
VILLA D'OR
FOLGATE LANE
COSTESSEY, NORWICH
NR8 5DP
TEL: NORWICH (0603) 743667

Now I have arrived home I have had a chance to have a good look at the lovely horse shoe you made for me. I did enjoy Watching you make it. I have seen pictures of black smiths at work. You are the First real blacksmiths I have seen. I am Keeping my horse shoe a sercet. Once again Thank You.

Yours sincerely

Sarah Lambirth

81. John is extremely proud of the forge and mill, which have a four-hundred year history behind them and although the blacksmith's is a fully working concern, he always welcomes school visitors and other interested parties who wish to see the ancient craft being performed. A typical letter of appreciation is reproduced here from a young lady from as far away as Norwich!

82. This is a more recent external photograph of the Mill Forge and Blacksmiths shop. On the roof for all to see is a superb weather vane, depicting two blacksmiths at work, another fine example of the professional standards that John West sets.

OLD MILL AND FORGE YSTRAD MYNACH

Chris Griffin 78

83. A delightful pen and ink drawing of the mill and forge as seen through the eyes of Chris Griffin in 1978. Some significant dates that are known concerning the building include - 1721 the first recorded date of a mill at Ystrad Mynach, used for grinding cereal for local farmers - 1729 the first positive evidence of the mill appears on Emanuel Bowen's map as Llanbradock Mill, later changed to Llanbradach - 1841 Parish records state the first miller as being Thomas Richards and the name now changed to Ystrad Mynach Mill - 1880 is the last record of any corn being ground here.

84. A special feature of the mill was its giant water-driven wheel, typical eighteenth century automation. This particular wheel was exceptionally large for the period, measuring 26 feet in diameter and twice the size of normal wheels to be found at the time. A tragic accident is recorded when the aforementioned Mr. Thomas Richards aged 52 was killed here due to the failure of an assistant miller to engage the safety device. The scarf which the gentleman was wearing became entangled in the machinery causing a horrendous death, the screams being witnessed by his wife who was waiting outside in a horse and trap whilst on their way to a local horse fair.

85. This section of a map from 1922 shows the location of the mill house and forge at Lower Ystrad Mynach, it being named as Melin Ystrad (disused). It is interesting to note that while the forge was in a disused state, there were another two such forges close by, one opposite the cooper's and one by the old bridge. Closer examination of the map with the assistance of a magnifying glass will reveal many more institutions and landmarks that have disappeared.

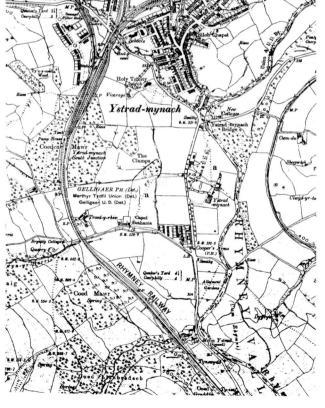

86. When this picture was taken of the postmistress outside Ystrad Mynach Post Office, the cost of posting a letter, which would have arrived the next day, was no more than ¹/₂p! The Post Office which stood on Caerphilly Road has naturally enjoyed a few alterations over the years but is still to be seen opposite the Ystrad Fawr and adjacent to the hospital. Mail collected from this office would be sorted and delivered by Hengoed's own sorting office in Raglan Road.

87. A view facing south at Hengoed Low Level station in about 1958 almost a hundred years after it first opened for passenger traffic. It was an important changing point for passengers wishing to journey on to Pontypool, Aberdare and Swansea and in early years travellers had a choice of first, second or third class travel. By comparison the first class fare to Cardiff was 13p return and 6p for a third class seat! A train service is still available from Hengoed but such a journey these days from Hengoed to the capital is best measured in pounds rather than pence.

88. The Great Western Railway Company's station at Ystrad Mynach as it looked in the 1920s with railway staff and prospective passengers posing for the cameraman. Gas lighting on the valley stations was the order of the day, part of the porters' duties being to light up each evening and extinguish after the last train.

89. A well-composed photograph of members of the GWR staff at Hengoed station suggesting that the porters might be in smart uniforms, ticket and office staff without the usual headgear and the stationmaster in his senior position at the front. A few of the staff seen here include Mr. Ballenger, Thomas Morgan, Frank Porter and Harold Pennells.

90. Mr. Albert Keeble is pictured here with a colleague at the exit from the High Level station. Four generations of the Keeble family worked on the railways namely Bob, a son also named Bob, his son Victor and his son Kevin. Bob Keeble as a young man started as a shunter in Newport Docks before transferring to Fleur De Lys. Further transfers took place in the direction of Hengoed and Bargoed from where he retired after many years service.

91. An additional view from the up platform of Maesycwmmer station, this time also showing the signal box.

92. A steam-hauled passenger train stands at the platform of Hengoed High Level in the 1950s when it was possible to have a choice of direction in which to travel. The options here were to continue on the Pontypool to Neath line or change for all stations within the Rhymney Valley.

93. This is a gathering of Ystrad Mynach apprentices together with their skilled trainers and supervisors around 1948-49. They were part of a government scheme to train future plumbers, carpenters, painters, bricklayers and electricians of which there was a shortage after the war. Employed by Gittins the builders, the picture was taken in Central Street Ystrad Mynach. Amongst the crowd are Colin Walters, John Edmonds, Bren Jones, Len ?, Wilf Hill, Dennis Ganderton, Jimmy Cullen, Alan Thomas, Brian Gibbs, John Jenkins, Tommy Owen, George Feast, Ross Powell, G. Williams and Mr. Symonds. Special mention must be made of John Edmonds (front first left) who was conscripted into national service and posted to Korea where war broke out in 1950 from which he did not return. His death was somewhat of a mystery when his well-armed patrol of eight soldiers went in search of the enemy in a paddy field but only seven were to return with no trace of their colleague. The disappearance was never explained; there being no enemy contact, the report could only read as *'missing in action'*.

CHAPTER 5

Religious Beliefs

94. Holy Trinity Church at Ystrad Mynach, the building of which began in the year 1855.

95. A wider view of the church and its burial ground, a view from the 1950s or early 1960s. Prior to the building of this fine stone Gothic styled construction, the only place of Anglican worship was a private chapel in Ystrad Fawr which was built under the guidance of Reverend George Thomas in 1843. It was the estate of Rev. Thomas that helped provide the finances needed for Holy Trinity which started in 1855 and took almost two years to complete. The foundation stone was laid by George William Griffiths Thomas, son of Rev. Thomas and the final costs were said to be in the region of £3700 - a mammoth sum. For the parishioners however it was a great deliverance, the building consisted of a chancel, nave, transept, a distinctive tower containing a peel of bells and seating for 140 souls. A few interesting notes available relating to the church include a sad memorial service held there on 29th January 1915 to mourn Mr. Charles Price, the first soldier from Ystrad Mynach to be killed in World War One. That war was also marked by great celebrations of peace in July 1919 the event being recorded as the biggest ever held in the parish. In the 1930s royal patronage was received from the Duchess of York (The Queen Mother) when she donated a Royal Doulton tea service as a prize in the church fête - the lucky winner was Mr. W.G. Farmer the local dairyman. In 1993 the church bells fell silent for the first time since 1945 caused by an unexpected catastrophe. Father Malcolm Davies was quietly listening to the radio programme *'The Archers'*, the particular episode referring to the church bells at *'Ambridge'* which had suddenly fallen through the roof, this prompting him to go and check his own bells at Ystrad Mynach church. The scene he found was one of despair and was obviously going to be an extremely expensive matter to put right and urgent advice was sought. The work was carried out by Mr. Trevor Bailey of White Chapel Foundry, ably assisted by Mr. Mark Rawlings and Mr. Andrew Berry with Mr. Derrick Packer recording the progress photographically. Photographs were sold in aid of the restoration fund, parishioners organized fund raising events and with many donations received, even from overseas resulting in a target figure of £2,000 being met in just one year.

96. An anxious moment is recorded for posterity whilst one of the bells is being lowered in place by Mr. Trevor Bailey of White Chapel foundry aided by Mark Rawlings and Andrew Berry, the culmination of a year's hard fund raising by so many followers.

97. Some members of the choir have time for a photograph outside Holy Trinity Church and some faces to look out for include Gerwyn Jones, Cerys Jones, Cecil Price, Tudor Jenkins (organist), Rachel Fine, Angela Boyland, Alex Creel and Father Florence.

98. Before Nonconformist worshippers could afford to pay for chapels of their own, it was common practice to hold their meetings and services in private homes or wherever they could find a suitable venue. The photograph above is of King's Hill Methodist Chapel as seen in 1936 and before this was built, meetings were held above William and Harriet Evans's shop, they being bakers and shop owners in Brynavon Terrace. A great benefactor to local religious causes was Mr. Joseph of the famous Rank Organisation and it was he who provided more than half of the funds needed to construct the chapel in King's Hill. Wherever people like William and Harriet bought flour for their bakeries, Rank would help in the building of a chapel in that town or village. There are in fact a number of Methodist chapels in the Rhymney and Rhondda valleys that were financed by Joseph Rank.

99. King's Hill sisterhood in 1951 and the group is gathered for the retirement of Mr. and Mrs. Argyle. Some names to be remembered are - 1st Row: Mrs. Oliver, Mr. and Mrs. Argyle and Mrs. Eskley. 2nd Row: Mrs. Preston, Mrs. Rowlands, Mrs. Brown, Mrs. Thomas, Mrs. Price, Mrs. Wilson, Mrs. Smart, Mrs. Roberts, Mrs. Cornick, Mrs. Day, Mrs. Webb, Mrs. Roles, Mrs. Holland, Mrs. Jones and Mrs. Emms. 3rd Row: Mrs. Morgan, Mrs. Piper, Mrs. Gordon, Cissy Oliver, Mrs. Bowen and Mrs. Jones. 4th Row: Mrs. Brooks, Mrs. Davies, Mrs. Williams, Mrs. Vaughan, Mrs. Ireland and Mrs. Pugh.

100. Hengoed Baptist Chapel, a place of ancient worship. The chapel stands on a hilltop overlooking Ystrad Mynach and has a fine view of the whole valley, looking down towards Caerphilly in one direction and Gelligaer mountain and the Beacons in the other. From the back of the church there is a view of another mountainous landmark, that of Mynyddislwyn.

The original chapel was built as early as 1710, a building described as being made of stout oak, measuring 40 feet by 20 with two stables and all for a cost of around £300. As the congregations gathered in number, larger premises were necessary and a new chapel was opened on 11th October 1829. To worship in this place, members would have travelled from far and wide and on horseback if lucky enough. Local lady Dilys Stemp recalls her mother Iris May telling of one fine lady who used to ride to chapel at the turn of the century, always acknowledging her; Iris herself having plenty of walking to do from Brithdir to Cefn Hengoed to work at Dorkins's farm.

Baptisms in the early years would have taken place in the Rhymney River and the Cylla Brook which is just a short walk away. A more comprehensive history of Hengoed Chapel may be found in the work *'The New Hengoediana'* or *'The History of Hengoed Baptist Church'* by Morgan Edmonds which details the persecutions carried out in the district against the Nonconformists and how they would be dragged out of their beds at night to face punishment for their beliefs.

101. The dedicated members of the sisterhood belonging to Zoar Presbyterian Church Maesycwmmer are pictured on the church steps. Old Zoar church was built in 1863 being situated at the top end of Maesycwmmer and to be seen in this photograph are - Mrs. Arthur, Mrs. Jones, Mrs. Walters, Mrs. John, Mrs. Evans, Mrs. Davies, Mrs. Margaret Jones, Mrs. Edith Jones, Mrs. Prothero, Mrs. Nancy Lewis and Mrs. Davies.

102. This is a large crowd of pupils and their teachers at Cefn Hengoed in the 1930s when the rooms of No.30 Gelligaer Road were used for Sunday School lessons. Many of the names have been given - Oliver Williams, Canon Williams, Sister Jones, Ms. Winwood, Rene Evans, Twin James, Ms. Casley, Cridwen James, Ms. Winwood, Olwen Wood, ? James, Eunice Powell, Tilly Hammond, ?, Dilla Baines, Jimmy Fowler, ? Skinner, ? Brownette, Sadie Morgan, Dora Wood, Ian Lewis, Annie Dale, Sybil Stook, Violet Baines, Maudy Williams, ? Smith, Elsie and Ronnie Fowler, Lilian Wood, Gert Selwood, Twin James, Tommy Townsend, Maisie Townsend, Audrey Price, Brenda Price, Billy Baines, Desmond, Louis and Beryl Stook and ? Evans.

103. An excellent photograph of Tuckers Chapel taken in 1920, a chapel that once stood on top of Hengoed Avenue and The Crescent Cefn Hengoed. This chapel saw a number of uses over the years, particularly as a *'soup kitchen'* to feed the hungry during times of industrial unrest in the area. Other local inhabitants might have known it more familiarly as *'the chapel in the moonlight'*, it being a favourite spot for romantic moonlight views over the valley. A few names appearing in this picture include Mr. Tucker, Mr. Price, Tommy Haywood, Jack Chidgey, Mr. Townsend, Mr. Hinwood, Mr. Jarman, Mr. Bayliss, Mr. Whitock, Phil Court, Dan Hughes, Charlotte Hughes, M. Griffiths, Will Vivian, Sid Way and Mr. Greening.

104. A picture of *'Tucker's Fairies'* Cefn Hengoed taken outside the old school house Gelligaer Road and the children of the founder Mr. Tucker. Back Row: Willie Jones, Ivy Hammond, Eva Stemp, Tibby Roberts, John Smith, Ms. Jepson, Gwladys Jones, Ceinwen Young and Willy Anthony. Middle: Marge Powell, Millie Smith, Gwladys Evans, Elsie Davies, Violet Price, Hedley Tucker, May Newton, Lilian Tucker, Monica Tucker, Doris Haycock and Renee Price. Bottom: Rachel Davies, Violet Hammond, Jenny Eynon and Maud Young.

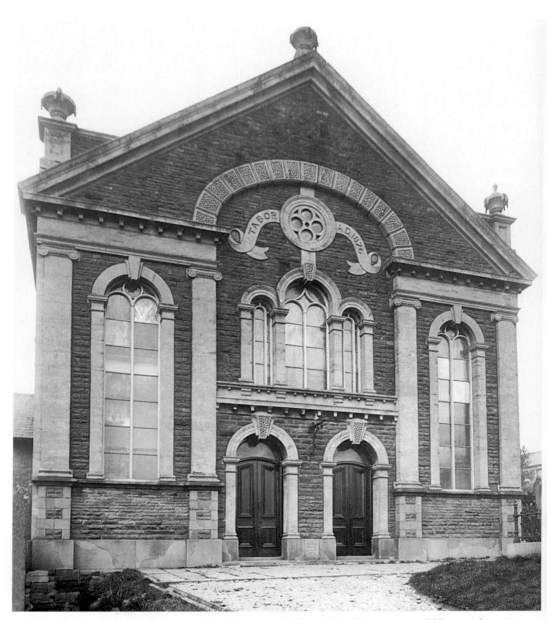

105. Tabor Chapel (the present vestry) was built in 1829 by a group of Nonconformists as an Independent or Congregational Church, its earliest minister also serving New Bethel, Mynyddislwyn. As the membership increased over the years, the building was considerably enlarged, doubling its capacity by 1855. Even this was not enough and the decision was taken in 1876 to erect the much larger chapel as seen here with Reverend T.J. Hughes at the helm. Rev. Hughes, who had done so much to ensure the building of Tabor died in 1920 and both he and his wife lie buried in front of their beloved chapel. Some later ministers whose names may be remembered include Joan Jenkins (1930-44), Frank Saville (1945-48) and Gerald Smith (1956-64). In 1971 Tabor elected to join the United Reform Church and in 1996 became part of the Rhymney Valley VRC Pastorate (joining Bethany, Ystrad Mynach and Van Road Caerphilly) with Rev. Shelagh Pollard as pastor.

106. Siloh Church in Oakfield Street Ystrad Mynach. The beautiful rhododendron of Siloh was a prominent feature for many years, its bloom winning the admiration of many although now replaced by an ornamental garden. This church was opened in 1910, the creation of local builder Mr. George Davies and costing £950 at the time. Siloh was built to cope with the rapid expansion of the village of Ystrad Mynach, the existing Bethania, Lower Ystrad being a little remote for much of the growing population. With two places of worship then available, services were divided between them, alternating weekly with morning services held at Bethania and evenings at Siloh. To ensure that the young were indoctrinated into the faith, Sunday School was provided regularly by both churches.

107. The Gospel Hall Davies Street, of which the founder member was a Mr. L.H. Tranter who was resident at Hengoed House for a period. Prior to the building of the hall, regular meetings were held in the doctor's surgery in Park Road Hengoed until the members built their own premises seen here, opening for meetings in May 1921. Local resident Mr. Keen recalls that following the ever popular Whitsun walks, teas and games were held in Dan Herbert's field near the viaduct, where the main attraction for everyone was a large rope swing!

108. This photograph provides the opportunity for early members of Moriah Chapel, Bedwlyn Road to show their theatrical skills during their presentation of *Cinderella and The Prince* in the 1920s. A few names to recall are Katy Richards, Betty Phillips, ? Owen, Evan Evans, Peggy Roberts and Frances Evans.

109. Moriah has recently gone through some major renovations and is now known as Moriah Full Gospel Fellowship. The pastors Andrew and Linda Taylor, with the help of some of the congregation, place great faith in their *'upper room project'*, which is dedicated to the younger members, youth being the key to a strong family unity in the church; even the youngest of members are catered for, with one of the four upper rooms being converted into a creche. In this picture from a 1950s outing to Barry Island are Mrs. Richards, Katy Richards, Eunice Williams, Susan Richards and Lindsey Gwynn.

CHAPTER 6

Schooldays

110. Hengoed Board School. Hengoed Infants' School was first opened on August 1st 1887 and continued to provide education for the community through two world wars until it was closed due to fire damage during the summer holidays of 1973. The picture seen here is of Mr. John Lewis the headmaster sitting in his study in the year 1915.

Below are a few interesting extracts from the headmaster's log book during the first days of service in 1887.

August 1st	This school was opened with the following staff: Jane Hopkins (Certified Teacher). Margaret Cross (Monitress). Elizabeth Rees (Ditto). Forty-four children admitted, 20 boys and 24 girls. Mr. Edwards and Mr. Lewis called in.
August 2nd	Six more children admitted today 5 boys and 1 girl.
August 9th	New total now 70, 32 boys and 38 girls. The formal opening of the school took place this afternoon, after which the children were entertained with buns and ginger beer.
August 12th	Scarlet fever is raging in a few houses in the neighbourhood, three children from families infected have been prevented from coming to school.
August 22nd	New books received.

111. The cookery class in the school in 1915 in days when it was thought necessary to educate females only, in the art of cooking and chalked on the blackboard for all to see are the following instructions for the preparation of 'Grilled Fish.

1.   Stoke a clean bright fire free from smoke.
2.   Heat griller and grease with suet.
3.   Trim and wash fish, wipe and coat with seasoned flour.
4.   Place in hot griller and cook on one side until golden brown.
5.   Turn with knife and spoon (never use a fork), cook on other side until brown.
6.   Serve with chips and sauce.
7.   Small cutlets take 7-10 minutes to cook.

112. Another scene from the interior of the school with the boys class at their wooden desks watched over by the headmaster and teacher. Today's pupils will have to use a little imagination to appreciate classroom conditions some ninety years ago such as gas lighting, chalk and slates instead of pen and paper and a good thrashing from 'sir' for the slightest misdemeanour!

113. Hengoed Junior School in the 1950s and here are some names to look out for - Back: Mr. D.J. Owen, Andrew Costa, Howard Lane, David Blackwell, Malcolm Langley, Jeffrey Rodway, Ken Pascoe, Alan Mills, Eugene Marriott, Geoffrey Holder and Mr. Hayes. Middle; Mansel Dainton, Douglas Moore, Hayden Ruck, Melvin Davies, Gerald Jones, Emlyn Webb, Trevor Court, John Llewellyn and Daffyd Jones. Front: Jennifer Jones, Betty Bishop, Siân Davies, Janet Campbell, Ruth George, Maria Cooper, June Boxendale, Barbara Gittins, Angela Roles, Phyllis Morgan and Betty Howells.

114. Another 1950s photograph from the Junior School and some more names are given as - Back: Mr. D.J. Owen, Gareth Hughes, Tony Costa, Neil Boardman, Lyn Hegarty, Ian Goodenough, Jeffrey Edwards, Graham Paget, Kenneth Cooper, Gareth Preece, Stuart Rowlands, Mostyn Williams. Middle: Lyn Coles, Brian Jones, Ieuan Rees, Mair King, Evelyn Davies, Verna Millsom, Joy Cooper, Michael Burgin, Robert Old, Phillip Mills, Mrs. Griffiths. Front: Carol Powell, Ann Rogers, Siân Gittins, Olwen Griffiths, Joyce Evans, Vicky Ellis, Christine Williams, Susan Amor, Susan Hellings, Trena Howells, Elizabeth Williams.

115. Some more pupils and teachers from the Junior School during the mid 1950s. Back: Mr. D.J. Owen, Alex Preece, Kerry Jones, Carl Jones, Brian Burton, David Davies, Steven Meyrick, Phillip Old, Ivor Blunt, Paul Butts, Noel Hughes, Dilwyn Rees, John Fletcher Davies and Teacher Mrs. Williams. Middle: David Everson, Gareth Luke, William Mallon, David Thomas, Royston Chapel, Graham Pearce, Phillip Christopher, Alan Thomas, John Stevens and Steven Thomas. Front: Mary Webb, Judith Millsom, Barbara Abbott, Pat Peters, Brenda Evans, Margaret Boucher, ?, Gina Carter, Pat MacDonald, Lynda Davies, Janice Woods and Wendy Morgan.

116. The years have moved a little for this junior school photograph and seen are - Back: Henry Williams, Gareth Everson, Paul Ireland, Gwyn Berrill, Michael Anthony, Peter Hopkins, Nigel Hart, Russel Davies, Timothy Davies and Teacher Mr. Cadwallader. Middle: David Baker, Richard Rogers, Angela Evans, Valerie Gittins, Lyndsey Peters, Shirley Jones, Gaynor Bowden, Cheryl Skidmore, Carol Williams, Kelvin Morris and Clive Price. Front: Lynette Jones, Gaynor Capper, Jane Spencer, Siân Greenaway, Julie Brown, Marina Rees, Tracy Shaddick, Christine Evans and Ann Mathews.

117. Some more familiar faces for former pupils to recall are - Back: Mr. D.J. Owen, Stuart Harmon, Mark Old, Gary Berrill, Alan Boobier, Alan Shires, Elwyn Rees, Damion Cushion, Steve Goodenough, David Holder, Marion Edwards, Howard Roles, Colin Thomas, Mrs. Price. Middle: Marilyn Payne, Angela Barber, Lorraine Smith, Suzanne Bowen, Ann Dolloway, Meryl Williams, Robert Jones, Martin Phillips. Front: Gaynor Taylor, Pamela Cooper, Kerry Holder, Janet Lewis, Karen East, Ann Spencer, Kathleen Bennett, Jane Mills, Sonia Woods, Andrea Williams and Gwenda Parry.

118. The 1961-62 term and some new faces have arrived at school - Back: Mr. D.J. Owen, Kevin Rees, Michael Mallon, Ian Duggan, David Evans, Gavin Sunderland, David Marsh, Roger Mills, Derek Roberts, Wynne Rudge and teacher Mrs. Griffiths. Middle: Ann Casley, Diane Roles, Lyn Coles, Alan Hellings, Joseph Jug, Jimmy Herold, Vanessa Carter, Pamela Chaplin. Front: Helen Lewis, Janette Macdonald, Janet Czaja, Marilyn Hughes, Marilyn Davies, Eira Jones, Jane Rogers, Ann Chivers, Jennifer Amor, Marlene Skidmore, Avril Bird, Siân Ascot.

119. Back to some earlier years now and probably 1956-57 - Back: Mrs. Pearce, Michael Lewis, John Pardoe, Alan ?, Tony Taylor, John Berrill, John Macdonald, Keith Garbutt, Christopher Bassett, Peter Nicholas, Alan Pardoe, John Herbert and Mr. Owen. Middle: Maldwyn Griffiths, Alan Edmunds, Elizabeth Peters, Gwendoline Greenaway, Theresa Courtney, Kathryn Robinson, ?, Avril Livings, Margaret Edmunds, Elwyn Eddington, Lynn Hegarty. Front: Lyn Price, Barbara Nicholas, Millicent Livings, Kathleen MacCallum, Elizabeth Williams, Susan Fox, Jacqueline Cox, Margaret Skidmore, Gloria Stone, Iris

120. This picture is from about 1959 and although some pupils's names have not been traced, the faces will still be familiar to many - Back: Teacher Mrs. Thomas, Brian Jones, Glyn Bishop, Alistair Sunderland, Richard Herold, Howell Luke, ?, Ieuan Rees and Mr. Owen. Middle: Jeffrey Edwards, Lloyd Edwards, Philip Gabriel, Alan Rudge, ?, Marlene Skidmore, Avril Thomas, Gary Bufton, Paul Hayter, Alan Jones, Kenneth Cooper. Front: Hilary Paget, Irene Moore, Ioal Davies, ? Williams, ?, Marilyn Gittins, Lyn Jones, Joyce Evans, Diane Jones, Kathleen George.

121. Cefn Hengoed Infants' School in the late 1950s and the names provided are as follows - Back: Clive Brooks, Keith Meredith, Brian Smith, Hedley Angove, John Greening, Alan Jones, Harry Ross, George Winwood, Robert ?, Gary Humphries. Middle: Michael Weyman, Ernie Holton, John Gibby, Eileen James, Jennifer Jones, Jacqueline Griffin, Collette Smith, Elaine Partridge, John Edwards, Tyrone Hinwood, Nigel/Alan Stenner. Front: Susan Vivian, Marlene Brownette, Sylvia Mathews, Gillian Bayliss, Veronica Smith, Pamela Smith, Julie Taylor, Sheila Poulton, Katherine Everson, Linda Phillips, Barbara Morris, Pauline Roberts and Sandra Wallbank.

122. Cefn Hengoed in 1957 with the following pupils and teachers. Back: Mrs. Jones, Brian Hart, Denise Sumner, Steven Collier, Albert Williams, Grant Stevens, Alan Ward, David Poulton, Robert Harding, John Ash, Tommy Haywood, Terry Thomas, Mr. Evans. Middle: Raymond Meredith, Donald Humphries, Barbara Atkinson, Ros Cuttliff, Jennifer Evans, Valerie Barber, Catherine Phillips, Pam Roberts, Hillary Delataste, Gary Jay, Idris George. Front: Rosemary Morris, Annette Davies, Marlene Bickham, ? Williams, Ruby Murray, Janet Hughes, ?, Evelyn Fowler, Ann Bowers, Helen Jones, Christine Selwood. Squatted are Les Smith, Mike Williams and Tommy Baker.

123. Cefn Hengoed School 1960-1961. Back: Dougie Mackenzie, Tony Humphries, John Dexter, ? Rees, Eddie Evans, Henry Smiga, Michael Weyman, Alan Stenner, Paul McCarthy, David Stevens, George Purnell. Middle: Andrew Edmunds, Jeff Thomas, ?, Veronica Smith, Elaine Partridge, Joyce Evans, Ellien Meara, Sheila Poulton, Pam Smith, Alan Price, Haydn Warburton, Kenny Lewis. Front: ?, Jean Brownett, Vanessa Jones, Ann Woods, Sylvia Mathews, Susan Vivian, Susan Powell, Gillian Bayliss, Ann Evans, Elaine Buckley, Pauline Roberts, ?.

124. Cefn Hengoed about 1959. Back: Les Pope, John Marshall, Mal Jones. Middle: Tommy Reeks, Robert Probert, Malcolm Brooks, Terry Brooks, Tommy Haywood, Clive Brooks, Michael Crockson, Donald Humphries, Tony Warburton. Front: Gillian Terry, Janice Griffiths, Meryl Sharp, Evelyn Fowler, Joyce Buckley, Barbara Atkinson, Elaine Williams, Val Young, Sandra Thomas, Kay Johnson, Maureen Wallbank. The teachers are Mr. Norman Reynolds and Mr. Evans.

125. Pictured here at City Hall Cardiff are the ladies of Lewis School Ystrad Mynach, the Headmistress at the time was Mrs. Hemmings. They were BBC School Choir runners up in 1991, a remarkable achievement in an event sponsored by British Gas Wales and BBC Cymru. Starting at the back, left to right are - Tanya Williams, Rhiannon Morgan, Emma Jones, Angela Kitchin, Sarah Taylor, Rhian Lewis, Alison Robins, Laura Joshi, Elizabeth Jones, ?, ?, Eluned Miles, ?, Suzanne Smith, Charlotte Grubb, Claire Nicholas, Claire ?, Maria Kitchin, Lorna Williams, Jessica Deeks, Kathryn Taylor, Rachel Griffiths, ?, Jessica Deer, Barbara Thomas, Leanne Jones, Sarah Williams, Natalie ?, Rebecca Williams, ?, Yvonne West, Bethan Jenkins, Kate Rees, Rhiannon ?, Catherine Morgan, Lianne Jones, Sarah Barnett, Elizabeth Grey, Elizabeth Cheeseman, Eleanor Whitman, Amy Williams, Catherine Drinkhall, Emma Jordan, Valerie James, Siân Schutz, Kate Hopkinson, Joanne Gwyther, Catherine Lee, Kelly Nottingham, Fiona Cule and Sarah Mallon.

126. This time it's the turn of Ystrad Mynach School to be pictured with most of the names given as follows - Back: Liam Kean, ?, ?, ?, Roger Jenkins, Ian White. 3rd Row: ?, Tony Saunders, John Maslen, Christopher Barnes, David Borowski, ?, ?, Mark Jenkins, Gary Manning. 2nd Row: Cynthia Thomas, Susan Parker, Alison Hillier, Jane Malpas, Sarah Packer, Christine Adams, Margaret Hopkins, Pauline Paget, Hillary Phillips, Ellen Perring. Front: Carol Lessimore, Siân Hester, Lynette Rees and Ann Morris.

127. It's back to the 1950s for this school photograph at Ystrad Mynach and seen are - Back: Kenny Davies, Malcolm Hester, Raymond Thomas, Ralph Darch, John Digby, Reggie Scrivens, ?, Jeffrey Mathews, Gary Kinstley. Middle: Siân Watkins, Judith Weeks, Pat Tudor, Nesta Thomas. Front: Wendy Evans, Valerie Penrose, Susan Richards, Margaret Drobisz, Christine Pugh, Vanda ?, Mary Ellis, Gillian Hector and Lindsay Gwynn.

128. An early picture of Hengoed School for Girls. The construction of this school began in 1899, the foundation stone being laid by Miss Prosser of Treharris on November 9th of that year. It took almost twelve months to complete and was officially opened on November 1st 1900 with Miss Winifred James as headmistress. Initially the school was planned for just eighty pupils but after some twenty years it was considerably enlarged, now catering for 350 girls. By the time the school closed in 1959 however, there were more than 500 on the register. After closure as a school, the building saw alternative usage for small industrial undertakings until finally being demolished in the 1980s.

129. Miss Richards and the school prefects in 1937-38. Many of the names are known such as Nesta Jones, Isabella Brick, Nancy Gurner, Doreen Tuck, Betty Jones, Glenys Crocker, Joan Sutton, Nancy Griffiths, Joy MacGregor, Christine Sketch, Edith Walters, Mary Williams, Molly Young, Margaret Thomas, Mary Llewela Williams, Eunice Price, Mary Gurner, Doreen Jones, Marion Jones, Audrey Morley ?, Marjorie Watkins, Mary Davies, D. Young, Edith Jones and Margaret C. Thomas. Nesta Jones (far left front row) later became Dept. Head Prefect and recalls the school being very strict and regimental in every way. After leaving school Nesta graduated from Cardiff University, teaching history at Cardigan, Pontypool and Ystrad Mynach Secondary School.

130. The Lewis Girls' Comprehensive School Ystrad Mynach and the Year 8 Hockey Team, coached by Miss Karen Jones proudly photographed after winning the National Urdd 2000 title. The players are - Back: Ffion Bishop, Katie Ruwerda, Rachel Davies, Siân Parker, Kim Eynon, Kirsty Philpots and Crissie Trueman. Front: Lisa Astley, Lucy Gould, Michelle Huber, Melanie Powell, Hannah Williams, Judy Harrington and Gemma Roberts.

131. Since the appointment of Dr. Sue Noake in 1996, Lewis school's achievements have grown from strength to strength always supporting the activities organized by Urdd, enjoying much success in their national hockey and netball competitions; the school in total has a lot to be proud of with academic successes in all departments. Above is the Under 16s netball team 1999 Welsh National Schools finals and the girls are - Back: Claire Davies, Jennifer Williams, Joanne Dimond, Samantha Jones and Gemma Davies. Front: Gemma Williams and Michelle Littlewood.

132. Probably from the late 1950s comes this school photograph at Ystrad Mynach with teacher Miss Truman on the right. Not all of the pupils' names have been traced but here are some of those included - Back: David Jones, Robert Jennings, Michael Edwards. Middle: Brian Greenaway, Michael Dobbins, Geoffrey Price, Jennifer Dunk, Anitza Scribitz, ?, David Inseal, Peter Payton, Phillip Lee. Front: Barbara ?, Christina ?, Rosalyn Perrott, Pamela ?, Wendy Payton, Linda Edwards, Rosina James, Gaynor Daniels, Janice Powell and Jennifer Hall.

133. Some more pupils to be spotted in this 1950s photograph include - Back: David James, Robert Jones, Phillip Dowell, Brent Perrott, John Lee. Middle: John Johnstone, Alan Hayter, Ricky Gillard, David Edwards, Gordon Morris, Marcus Ariallous, Richard Bufton, Mr. Pugh (Teacher). Front: Susan Teconi, J. Williams, Ann Penrose, Christine Walliner, ?, Madeline Lane, Barbara ?, J. Williams, Christine Taylor and Gaynor Haggett.

134. This picture from 1955 provides the opportunity for Maesycwmmer Junior School to be seen in print with their teacher Mr. Alf Probert on the left. The youngsters are - Back: Chris Griffin, Edward Harris, Rory Bright, Reginald Francis, David Evans, David E. Roberts, Ken Jones. Middle: Gerald Pugh, David J. Roberts, Diane Lewis, Avril Morris, Gwyneth Hatton, Maureen Picket, Jacqueline Gibbs, Mavis McPhearson, Ron Jones, Colin James. Front: Ann Cannon, Gloria Yemm, Christine Milton, Freda Weeks, Margaret Gwyther, Jean Morgan, Megan Nicholas, Andrea Jonathon, Ann Brideaux, Gillian Cobley and Susan Harris.

135. Pupils and their teachers outside Maesycwmmer School in about 1965 and in the picture accompanied by headmaster Mr. Howells and teacher Mrs. Perrott are - Back: Robert Jones, Lyndon Jones, Jeremy Marque, David Barwood, Yvonne East, Elaine Pritchard, Leighton Bishop. Third row: ?, Angela Baker, Clive Phillips, Alan Powell, Lesley Fear, Jonathan Farmer, Sandra Morgan and Steven Marshall. Second row: Clare Harding, Janet Fennell, Kay Saunders, Paul Zdzieblo, Brian Eales, Angela Chamberlain, Jane Brideaux. Front: Denise Jones, Kim Bryant, Marlene Bates, Susan Rees and Allison Luke.

CHAPTER 7
Sport and Entertainment

136. On the right is Dai Gardiner of Cefn Hengoed and in the world of professional boxing his is a name that will ring in everyone's ears. Dai has enjoyed sports all his life, his passion for boxing beginning at a very early age, after becoming NCB Champion at just 15. He then started with Ted Simms in Caerphilly before moving to Bargoed with Ray Gabriel; a much talented amateur with Bargoed ABC, he recorded 54 wins out of 68 fights. By 1962 he had become ABA Lightweight Champion, the year when he decided to turn professional with that other doyen of the boxing fraternity Eddie Thomas, in favour of an offered place in the Commonwealth Games. Unfortunately his career as a professional boxer was brought to a sudden halt when during a sparring session with Howard Winstone, the top rope snapped and Dai fell out of the ring breaking his back. After three months in hospital it was also found that he had a detached retina, thus enforcing an early retirement from the ring itself.

In 1965 however he took out a professional trainer's licence, following with a manager's licence in 1972. One of Dai's first champions was Johnny Owen, the British Bantamweight and European Champion, winning the Lonsdale Belt outright. As followers will know, Johnny of Merthyr Tydfil died tragically at the age of 24 during a fight with South American Lupi Pintor at the Olympic Stadium, Los Angeles in 1980. This event was to have a profound effect on Dai Gardiner leading him to turn his back on his beloved sport for the next three years.

When Dai did decide to return he went on to train and manage boxers such as Robbie Regan, European and IBF Champion, WBO Bantamweight Champion and outright winner of the Lonsdale Belt. Another great protégé was Steve Robinson, achieving WBO Featherweight Champion seven times, winning the European title and defending it, winning the World unconditional title, defending that on eight occasions. Dai's gym in Gelligaer has a full stable including Steve Robinson and a number of rising stars such as Enzo Maccarinelli and boxers like Chris Davies, Keith Jones with quite a few boys who are quite adequate enough to compete with anyone across the country. Mention must also be made of Dai Gardiner's grandson who is Welsh Schoolboys' Champion and friends such as Gary Thomas, Pat Chidgey, Kenny Harrison and Billy Summers who have been with him since the beginning, witnessing the influence he has on the youngsters of today.

It has often been said that Dai Gardiner is boxing in Wales nowadays, and not without foundation. Regarded as an inspiration to the young and a fatherly figure to his boxers, his mannerisms include paying their medical bills and refusing to accept any money from their first few fights arguing that they all deserve a chance in life whether they make it or not! In Dai's own words *'all the fighters I have had, and that is thousands I can count on my hand the ones who have gone astray'*. Even those who do not support his particular choice of sport, still marvel and appreciate his endless work for charities, helping deprived children and voluntary work with the mentally handicapped. Dai Gardiner, Boxer, Trainer, Manager, Matchmaker, promoter and true sportsman in every sense of the word!

137. One of the many highlights in Dai Gardiner's long career was Steve Robinson's WBO fight in 1993 and this picture shows the jubilation felt all around. The picture was taken moments after the fight was won and shows the champion being held high with his title belt by Dai Gardiner and Gary Thomas. This was a particularly hard fought title fight against John Davies, Robinson winning on points. Pat Chidgey seen standing on the left of the picture described it as a triumphant win for all concerned.

138. This final picture from the Dai Gardiner story is of the Welsh boxing team in 1965-67 when their opponents were some tough boys from the Armed Forces. Some names included are - Back: Dai Gardiner, Ray Dash (team manager), ? Pearce, John Wall, ?, ? Pearce, Albert Bartlett (team coach). Front: Geoff Pritchard, Patrick Mullins, ?, Johnny Owen and Michael Copp.

139. Bill Mills is another local inhabitant who has excelled in numerous sports and spent so much of his time in developing the talents of the young. He was a well-respected international badminton referee and in 1998 as an advanced senior coach, had taken charge of 21 tournaments including the Welsh International Championships. His list of sporting interests is lengthy and includes being a former table tennis player for the county, a football referee for 35 years and a keen batsman and wicket keeper for Pontllanfraith. Not to be forgotten too are the few half marathons in which he has participated and some good cycling work in aid of the blind, all at an age when many would have long faded into retirement.

140. Maesycwmmer United AFC have a number of important successes to their credit and this is a photograph taken when they won the West Gwent League title in 1973. In the picture are - Back: Ray Lawrence, S. Jenkins, E. James, D. James, P. James, John Cross, J. Evens, R. Skelding, M. Whatley, R. Cannan, J. Davies, D. Mote, T. Lewis, T. Johnson. Front S. Sanger, A. Davies, B. Poole, J. Dickson, D. Pugh, G. Davies, A. Davies, T. Davies with Robert Davies holding the cup.

141. The list of local sporting personalities who have achieved international fame continues with this picture of Hengoed's Ray Bishop. Starting in Bargoed YMCA, Ray was one of the St. Athan's five-a-side winners in 1968 (his fellow players were Billy Matthews, Mervin Woods, Brian Roberts and Wayne Gibbons). He was a Boys Club International playing against England and Scotland in 1973 and one of five players to play for Great Britain against Belgium. After playing for various clubs including Cheltenham, the talent spotters were soon to recognize his talents with Cardiff City snapping him up whilst in Division 2. Ray was renowned as a striker with penetrating pace from midfield and caught the opposing team out time and time again and during his time with the Bluebirds, he played 113 games scoring 31 goals. Ray and his brother Paul were both talented players who had been taught the skills from a very young age by their father, Ray senior.

142. The NCB Penallta under 16s team whilst area finalists in 1950, the team including Ray Bishop Snr. Some of the names are known as follows - Back: Ralph Price, Ron ?, Tommy Vivian, World Cup Ref. Mr. Griffiths, Ted Cook. Middle: Terry Frowen, Clive Pearce, Alan Williams, Georgie Collins, Mr. Sullivan (Penallta Manager). Front: Rowly Williams, Emrys Inseal, Terry Frowen Jnr. and Bill Flue.

143. On the left is yet another personality, Mel Davies who grew up in Hengoed (Hill View, the brown houses) with his parents and sister Rhiannon from 1953 to 1969. His wife Pat was raised in Heol Celyn (the next street), they both attending Hengoed Junior School. Mel was manager of one of the country's largest Job Centres in Cardiff until 1997 when he became the UK Director of Recruitment and Coaching for Challenger Sports, a large American soccer education specialist. Mel and Pat now recruit around 400 soccer coaches for summer camps across the USA, taking responsibility for coach training and orientation and all the other neccessities such as travel documents visas etc. etc. These involvements take up nine months of the couple's year, the remaining three months being spent in the USA, coach monitoring and preparation for the following recruitment season. Mel, a UEFA 'A' Licence coach also works part-time for Cardiff City as coach for their Under 17 team.

144. Pictured here is Shaun Robson champion hurdler on his way to winning a gold medal in an open race at Newport. He is another local sportsman to achieve so much including winning the Welsh Championships nine times and the Celtic twice, in the 110 and 400 metres hurdles and both 4 x 100 metres 4 x 400 metres. Shaun's success came after meeting Roy Richards, a sprint coach who happened to be at Bargoed during some track practise, this leading to meetings with Ivor Adams of Newport Harriers and the aim now is for a place in a Commonwealth Games team.

145. Long since retired, here is an Ystrad Mynach rugby team from 1949 with most of their names being recalled - Back: Morgan George, Gwillym Davies, Hywell Jones, Ernie Amor, Joe Jonathan, Jack Whittle, ?, Tom Evans, Stan Smith, J. Lessimore, Ivor Jones, Tommy Condick. Middle: Dennis Davies and George Davies. Front: Graham Whittle, John Richards, Vic Davies and Stuart Davies.

146. The lads of Graddfa School Ystrad Mynach have had many successes with their athletic teams, they being particularly noted for their team displays and this photograph from 1967-69 shows the following, some of the names are: Mel Hart, Paul Craven, ? Dunn, Mal Court, Elwyn Rees, Palmer. Middle: Phillip Salter, Colin Ludo, Leon Berrill, John Davies. Also Mr. Hughes, Mr. Osbourne, Mr. Rees, John Saunders, Colin Kirkham, Gareth Stockley and Steve Amos.

147. Time now for the game of cricket to get an airing with this photograph of part of an Ystrad Fawr team outside the pavilion in the park, the grounds being used extensively for a number of sports until the 1960s. Seen here are Eddie Jones, Bryn Thomas, Jack Lowe, Norman Price, Haydn Jarman, Tommy Gwillym and Steve Evans.

148. Skittles, which is a popular sport with many, and this is a picture of a triumphant Post Office team having just beaten arch rivals Caerphilly in 1978. Seen are Bert ?, Maldwyn Griffiths, Ken Hicks, Colin Thomas, John Jones, Geoff Holder, Ron Holder, Stan Spencer, Bob Carey, Benny Carey and Dilwyn Lewis.

149. Cefn Hengoed Pony Champions 2000. Members of Taff Fechan Pony Club enjoy the celebrations as winners of the Royal Windsor Horse Show Millennium Ride 2000 at Windsor Castle. As part of the celebrations they were allowed to ride through Windsor Castle grounds, the first to do so for a hundred years and they were presented with the Championship Cup and medals by H.R.H. Prince Phillip, an experience the riders will be unlikely to forget. In the photograph are Louise O'Brian, Richard Jones, Samantha Davies, Jody Whittle and Rebecca Davies.

150. Judo enthusiasts belonging to Ystrad Mynach A.T.C. in 1962. The 2352 Squadron team were the first cadets to appear at the Royal Albert Hall during a Festival of Remembrance and pictured here are Eugene Bowen, Jeff Matthews, Alan Harrigan, Mel Davies, Denis Summers, Brian Heffron and Lyn Baker.

151. This Penallta 1st team squad and committee members seen in the 1983-84 season after winning the district cup final against Wattstown RFC at Rhydfelin. The line up is as follows - Back: Bill Beer, Gary Morgan, Len Hatcher, Paul Rogers, Paul Ferris, Garnet Price, Lee Acreman, Bob Griffin, Mike Williams, Dai Flanagan, Craig Phillips, Colin Powell, Steve Tucker, Mike Guilfoyle, Brian Cornes, Nigel James, Ponty Jones, Neil Roberts, Mike Thomas, Tyrone Bullock, John Davies. Front: Alan Lintern, Wayne Jones, Jeff Davies, Butch Osborne, Leighton John, Dai Edwards (coach), Steven Jayne, Redfus Thomas, Mark Griffiths and Graham Munkley.

152. Penallta RFC (sponsored by Ruggabug) was placed firmly on the map of rugby football by winning the Welsh District Worthington Cup in 2001, beating Beaufort at the Millennium Stadium Cardiff 36-19. To add to this were further victories in the Rhondda and East Glam League and the Keith Jones District, making it a season to remember. The victors seen here are - Back: L. John, J. Davies, S. Tucker (coach), M. Oliver, M. Williams, N. James (manager), J. Griffiths, S. Lock, H. Stevens, G. Davies. Middle: M. Rowe, N. Thomas, D. Powell, R. Webber, I. Smith, M. Cook, G. Price, L. Acreman. Front: J. Hollifield, A. Powell, C. Johnson, R. Scrivens, S. Richards (captain), D. Hooper, D. Davies, J. Parfitt and R. Rowe.

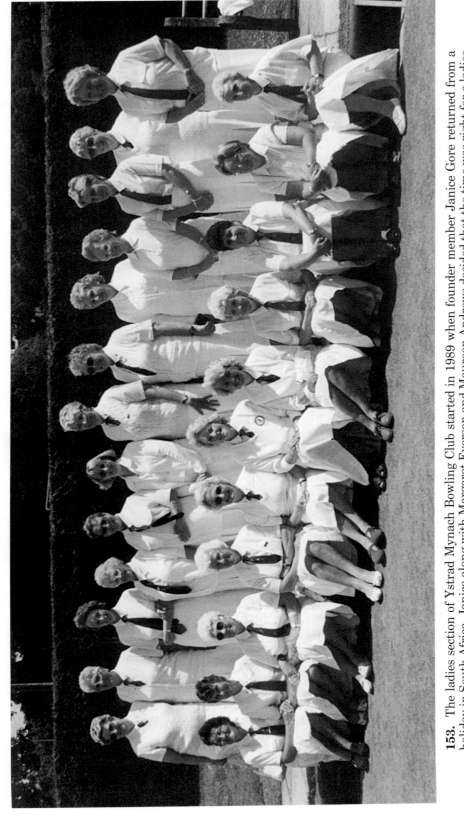

153. The ladies section of Ystrad Mynach Bowling Club started in 1989 when founder member Janice Gore returned from a holiday in South Africa. Janice along with Margaret Everson and Maureen Andrews decided that the time was right for a ladies section in this ancient sport. As part of their tenth anniversary celebrations, a fun game of bowls was arranged with a knockout tournament with dinner to follow and this is a photograph from the event. Back: June Wells, Margaret Everson, Margaret Knight, Pam Cook, Gloria Richards, Nesta Hadley, Barbara Taylor, Eira Morgan, Glenys Maslen, Audrey Davies, Pam Penrose (club sec.), Maureen Andrews, Thelma Sexon. Front: Jean Williams, Gwendoline Morgan, Joan Steel, Kath Poulton, Eunice Gore (club president), Margaret Davies, Pam Davies, Maureen Box, June Elsworth, Norma Noone, Melvis Edwards.

94

CHAPTER 8

Personalities and Events

154. Whilst not all of the names have been traced on this occasion, they will be remembered when they were members of the Cefn Hengoed Girls' Choir as seen here in 1968. Janice Hopkins (Wilding) recalls days when the choir would perform in local chapels and as a mark of appreciation, chapel members would take the girls to their homes for a tea party. Some of the names given are - Cled Williams, Sylvia Wallbank, Maria Gibby, Teresa Gibby, Susan Williams, Maureen Meredith, Janet Poulton, Mr. Sheen, Mr. Greenaway, Mrs. Williams, Jane McCarthy, Betina Vaughan, Karen ?, Susan Watkins, Lynette Davies, Susan Price, Wendy Jones, Carol and Valerie Holton, Janet Wilding, Joan Woods, Cheryl Roberts, Teresa Williams, Julie Grymel, Carol and Glynys Selwood, Yvonne Price, Maureen and Carol O'Donnell, Tina Roberts, Lyn and Cheryl McCarthy and Lynette Davies.

155. Some more choristers pose for the camera at Cefn Hengoed Hall; the choir was formed in 1943 as part of the ladies friendship club that met in the village hall. They entertained many audiences throughout the valley, singing occasionally with the Bargoed Male Voice Choir and many fine artistes and entertainers. Some of the founder members of the choir may be remembered such as Nancy James, Desi Smith and Gwen Oliver. Amongst the choir in this picture are Back - ?, ?, Betty Thomas, ?, ?, Alice Williams, Mrs. Oliver, Edie Young. Middle - Nancy Williams, Lolly Baines, Peggy James, Cridwen Rogers, Winnie Williams, ?, Nan Williams, Ollie Jones, Margaret Williams. Front - Ivy Edwards, Mrs. Noonan, Desi Smith, ?, Myfanwy Hughes, Bill Price, Peggy Lewis, Eileen Swithin and Sheila Williams.

ソプラノ 豊田喜代美

156. Ystrad Mynach Male Voice Choir was formed in 1965 by a group of friends who used to meet regularly on an informal basis at the Beech Tree Hotel and the choir has the distinction of being the first amateur Welsh choir to make a tour of Japan. The tour, sponsored by the Hitachi Corporation was a resounding success visiting a number of Japan's major cities including the capital Tokyo. The choir is pictured here at Caerphilly in 1979.

157. *'The Meteors'* was a band not to be missed during the 1960s. Formed in 1962 they were resident group at the Boys' Club as it was then known in Ystrad Mynach, together with another local band *'The Stompers'*. Readers of this book who are now probably in their fifties, will recall the band's professional rendering of hits by Chuck Berry, The Rolling Stones and of course The Beatles provided by Geoff Holder (vocals), Graham Pearce (rhythm guitar), Philip Old (bass guitar), Barry Jones (lead guitar) and Dave Thomas on drums.

158. *'The Stompers'* who formed the other resident band at the Boys Club were equally as popular as their counterparts, entertaining fans around the valley and beyond. They too were formed in 1962 during the great British *'pop revival'*, a speciality being their version of *'It's All Over Now'* by The Rolling Stones. The group members were Clive Brooks on drums, accompanied by Ken Pope, Gwyn Lewis, Danny Ross and John Edwards on the rhythm section.

159. During the 1940s and 1950s when dance orchestras were at their peak, the one to listen to locally was The Aneurin Thomas Collegians who were very popular in the valley and Gwent area. The orchestra is seen here during an evening at The King's Head Newport with their leader and amongst the many are Ray Thomas (drums), Dennis Jones (piano) and George Protheroe.

160. *'The Byron Jones Big Band'* which has been described by many as the finest big band to come out of Wales for many a year. Leader Byron Jones was brought up in Lewis Street Ystrad Mynach and took to music at an early age, playing trombone and fortunate enough to be a member of Aneurin Thomas's Orchestra mentioned above. Following numerous visits to the Brecon Jazz Festival, he was prompted to form his own band collecting the best talent he could find and being surprised at the amount and quality of jazz musicians in Wales. Now regulars at Brecon Jazz and receiving glowing write-ups in the national press, their ultimate venue is claimed to be *'Aberflyarff Stute'* immortalised by that great cartoonist *'Gren'* who will receive mention later.

161. A local band of alternative rhythm *'The Red and White's Jazz Band'* as seen here during the 1940s and in the picture are - Glyn Vivian, Les Court, John Jay, John Hughes, Selwyn Morgan, Billy Bullock, Dilwyn Phillips, Billy Elliott, Wilf Young, Dogga Jones, Joe Wilding, Glyn Terry, Dai Williams, Edgar Maine, Harry James, Ted Humphries, Cled Williams, Arthur Price, George Jay, Jim Fowler, Ted Terry, Denzil Phillips. The drummers are Ronnie Caroll, Louis Stook, Harry Vivian, Ivor Young and Glyn Griffiths.

162. Further back in time, now to the 1930s and another favourite group called *'The Picadors'* from Cefn Hengoed are pictured in full uniform. Only two names can be remembered unfortunately, John Jay and a Mr. Hammond but one of their little claims to fame was that on one occasion the Lord Mayor of Cardiff visited Cefn Hengoed and gave member Owen Matthews half a crown (12$\frac{1}{2}$ pence) as they were the only jazz band to have a mascot!

163. And so we come to *'Gren'*, a household name for the past 32 years to thousands especially to those who read the South Wales Echo and look forward to his daily cartoon feature. Grenfell Jones was born in Hengoed (the viaduct often featuring in his cartoons), and his work has earned international acclaim for his sporting calendars, work with 24 books and illustrations for many others including Max Boyce's best-seller *'I Was There'*. For his charitable work Gren has been honoured by the Variety Club of Great Britain and was to receive the MBE in 1991 for his services to the newspaper industry. He is remembered by many during his school and sporting days including Byron Jones, Ray Bishop and Roy Evans who recall Gren being the first player to have yellow football boots! Known as *'banana boots'* they were a novelty at the time, real pig skin boots brought all the way from South America by his brother Ray and also a real leather ball. As Gren now recalls *'having your own football gave you an air of importance as you could then easily become captain and select your own team'*.

164. This is a very familiar face in Ystrad Mynach, that of Billy Bennett who has been cutting hair in the town for more than fifty years and still not considering retirement even at the age of 73. His introduction to the trade began in days when gentlemen would pay a visit to the barber's for a shave, Billy working during the evenings and weekends lathering up their faces in readiness. Having left school at 14 he took up a hairdressing apprenticeship in Gilfach, where after three years of training his wages had risen to a princely 53 pence a week! After conscription as a *'Bevin Boy'* for four and a half years at Britannia Colliery, the urge to trim hair returned and he worked for Ken Powell in Lower Penallta Road for about seven years before finally starting his own business in 1957 at *'Lancey's Corner'*. This is where he will be found today, still cutting hair at 1990 prices and sharing all the local news and events to the delight of his loyal customers.

165. Here is another well-known face and hairdresser of the district, Ray Lawrence. Ray started as an apprentice with Constantinou's Cardiff in 1963 and after completing the training, he opened his own salon in Maesycwmmer in 1965, later moving to Ystrad Mynach in 1987. Always involved in many things local, the list is extensive and includes Sec. of Lewis Boys P.T.A. 1983-86, founder member and chairman on several occasions of Maesycwmmer Utd., the now defunct Viaduct Utd. and a year's chairmanship of Tredomen Welsh League Football Club.

166. It was some nine years after the end of the First World War before the district had its own memorial erected to honour the fallen, in 1927. The unveiling ceremony is recorded in this picture with Bishop Timothy Rees on the right and Reverend W.J. Williams in front of the monument. The memorial now stands in the grounds of Ystrad Fawr Council Offices but prior to there being such a cenotaph at all, Mrs. Mary Roberts (nee Davies) of Ystrad Mynach recalls when in the girl guides, the annual armistice parade would march through the town to lay wreaths on a lamppost at the foot of the pier head building.

167. Some of the girls from Cefn Hengoed and Ystrad Mynach who worked at the munitions factory in Cardiff docks during the Second World War. Sylvia Carroll (nee Vivian) recalls a most jovial atmosphere amongst the girls as they produced a variety of dangerous weapons. This photograph was taken in Queen Street Cardiff whilst on their way to work with - Back: Sally Selwood, Phyllis James, Violet Jane. Front: Sylvia Vivian, Lil James and Esther Griffiths.

168. Continuing with the active service theme, this is Charlotte Greenaway from Cefn Hengoed who was a founder member of the Women's Royal Flying Corps in 1917. After the war ended in November 1918, Charlotte was to work for a number of charities selling poppies and flags etc. in aid of the veterans. One notable event at the time was when there was a slight misunderstanding regarding authorization to sell these items, but such was the concern when the mistake had been discovered, the RAF saw fit to send a high ranking officer armed with a suitable and humble apology accompanied by a police escort!

169. In the nicest possible way, the gentleman pictured here was otherwise known as *'Mad Morgan'* from Ystrad Mynach. When Elaine Morgan sat down with her father to hear of his war-time experiences, little did she realize that she would be spending the next twelve months writing his biography for publication. The book gives a moving account of Reginald Morgan's life through harrowing times of poverty, two world wars, the 1930s Depression and how he earned the title Mad Morgan through his daredevil wartime dispatch riding. Reg was also caught up in politics when during a dispute between two trade union factions, he became involved in a strike underground and a confrontation with some overseers. He was struck on the head by a spanner and after regaining consciousness, just managed to crawl to safety from a journey of trucks which certainly would have caused a fatality.

170. A relaxed photograph of Ron and Peggy Holder that has another tale to tell, they being married in November 1941 just before Ron was posted overseas to serve in the war. In an unlikely twist of fate during the Pearl Harbour situation, his ship was diverted to Java and whilst there, was taken off a transportation truck to make way for an injured soldier. Unfortunately this event had dire consequences for he was soon taken prisoner by the Japanese and it was some eighteen months before news was received of his whereabouts, having been presumed lost in action. For Ron and his family there were four agonising years before he was eventually released in 1945.

171. Luigi and Elvira Bracchi pose happily with their mother Maria in their café in Bedwlyn Road. The family relates that things were extremely hard in the early days and making ice cream by hand was an arduous task indeed. Their father Giovanni and uncle Luigi constructed an early type freezer in the back of the café and would collect blocks of ice from Ystrad Mynach station, it having been sent up from Cardiff to be used as insulation packing.

172. Bruno and Rina Sidoli came to Wales in 1951 from Bardi in northern Italy with Bruno working in the coal industry and Electricity Board before setting up the family business in Cillfynydd, later moving to Ystrad Mynach in 1965. The café is now run by son John and his wife Meryl with Rina lending a hand when needed. John is known to be a great Meccano enthusiast with models on display in the café along with lots of other memorabilia which he has collected over the years and are of great interest to the customers.

173. A proud John Massari of the Central Café Ystrad Mynach pictured in his Royal Artillery uniform during the 1939-45 war, he suffering a shrapnel wound to his leg whilst relying on wife Lena to carry on the business. Active in the British Legion and Chamber of Trade, John together with Mr. Guppy the butcher and Mr. Mason the dentist have also been kind to the Boys Club, donating a snooker table.

174. Mrs. Basso and some pupils of her Italian class, which she successfully ran for twenty years at Lewis Girls' School from 1975 to 1995. As well as Italian lessons there were cookery lessons too and pictured here are an Easter dove cake and some traditional espresso coffee. In the picture are Mrs. Nita Basso, Marie Packham, Hayley Carter, Florence Sparham, Maria Williams, Katie ?, Harriet Jones and Dina Sidoli.

175. When Mr. Alan Morgan of Hengoed first started collecting postcards, little did he realize how much time, effort (and money) the hobby involves. Now living in Maesycwmmer, he has built up an extensive collection over the years, emphasizing on views of the Rhymney Valley and its long history: Alan has kindly loaned some of his treasured material in the compilation of this book.

176. Yet another local inhabitant with definite skills is Stuart Holloway. A great motorcycle enthusiast he could often be seen competing at Pendine Sands and a staunch member of Gilfach Triangle Motorcycle Club. Stuart who was a postman at Hengoed sorting office, could turn his hand to almost anything and when the office moved to new premises he used the building to make crossbows and is seen here perfecting one of his superior quality bows.

177. Here is a face that will be familiar to many not only locally but much further afield. This is Allan Rogers M.P. who was born in Penybryn and attended Glyngaer and Gelligaer Schools before graduating in geology at Swansea University. After working as a geologist in Canada, U.S.A. and Australia, he returned to Wales and embarked upon a career in politics, beginning with local council representation before ascending to the European Parliament and Labour Member for the Rhondda constituency at Westminster. A well respected parliamentarian who has not severed his links with very many matters of local interest, he is seen here with his wife Cridwen during a momentous occasion in 1990 whilst meeting Pope John Paul at a summer palace near Rome.

178. Graham Court O.B.E. is pictured here with Prime Minister the Rt. Hon. Tony Blair during his first public questions and answers session in Wales. The location was Llancaiach Fawr the historic building which was acquired for the borough council by Mr. Court with fellow councillors Wynn David and Mr. H. Edwards. Mr. Court received an award from the Prince of Wales committee for his efforts and the fortified manor, set in the heart of the Rhymney valley, is a superb example of 16th and 17th century architecture. The building is open to the public as a living history museum complete with visitor centre.

179. The whole of Griffiths Street Ystrad Mynach is out to celebrate the coronation of King George VI in May 1937 and amongst the many are David Porter, Mrs. O'Connor (former local shopkeeper), John Nicholas, Mrs. Rouse (laying-out nurse), Aneurin Paske, Mrs. M.A. Davies, Iris Nicholas, Mary Ann Ellis (shop), Ronnie Clifford, Joan Barnes, Mrs. Lucas, Audrey Woosnam, Trevor Horrell, Linda Horrell, Betty Woosnam, Eileen Rees, Mrs. M. Rouse, Mrs. R. Powell, Jessie Hart, Phyllis Oaten, Mr. W. Evans, Doreen Lucas, Chrissie Clifford, Don O'Connor, Mrs. G. Dolloway, Nancy O'Connor, Jean Lucas, Gwyneth Evans, Mrs. Dainton with Roy Winston and Arthur, Reene Rouse, Mrs. A. Kedward (nee Ellis), Edward O'Connor, Reg Wakefield, Mrs. Ellis (shop), Terry O'Connor, Don Rouse, David Rouse, Sammy Hart, Mrs. Everson, Margaret Williams, Doris Paske, boy Everson, Tom Phillips, Mrs. Jones, Phyllis Baines, Mr. and Mrs. Bill O'Connor and baby, Mrs. Evans senior, Mr. and Mrs. Trevor Bee and baby.

180. Mr. Bill Davies and other members of the postal staff are pictured being presented with their good driving awards outside Hengoed sorting office which was in Raglan Road in 1936. Mr. White, Cardiff head postmaster performed the ceremony and amongst the locals are Miss Ann Protheroe (left) postmistress sorting office, Ron Holder (2nd left and highly thought of postman) and Peggy Jones (right and later to become Mrs. Holder).

181. Here is one lucky gentleman surrounded by a fine bunch of girls who belong to Ystrad Mynach's Chamber of Trade during one of their annual outings in 1955, and amongst the numerous duties of the Chamber was that they were all enthusiastic in raising monies for charities. Some of the names known are Elvira Bracchi, Mrs. Lloyd (ironmongers), Gillian Edwards, Audrey Davies and Myfanwy Jones.

182. Another picture belonging to the Chamber of Trade as they pose during an annual dinner and dance held at the Institute Hall, the music being provided by the ever popular Aneurin Thomas and his dance band. The town's traders seen here are Emlyn and Lena Lloyd ironmongers, Evan and Llewela Richards undertakers, Steve and Gwen Evans ironmongers, Mr. and Mrs, Ivor Webb estate agent, Mr. and Mrs. Coppage butchers, Arthur and Eileen Williams London House Drapers, Mr. and Mrs. Phillips, Mrs. John and Miss Morgan.

183. Pictured is another Ystrad Mynach gentleman of considerable talent, Mervyn Burch who is seen with fellow composer Mark Morris at his Canadian home and planning another of their operas. Their work has been staged globally including South Africa where one of Nelson Mandella's grandchildren performed in the cast. Mervyn began playing the piano at five years of age and by the age of twelve was writing music for Lewis Boys School Choir; his career in music went on to include teaching at the Welsh School of Music, Bargoed Grammar and a long stay at Lewis Girls School. The latest composition portrays the plight of children in war, and numerous visits have been made to areas of conflict to understand their suffering. In 1991 Mervyn was presented with one of Wales's most prestigious music awards, The John Edwards Memorial Award for the promotion of Welsh Music.

184. The much admired Desi Smith of Cefn Hengoed who is always to be found at the heart of any charity work. She has devoted her entire life to helping those in need, being a founder member of the Ladies Social Club during the 1940s, to which her services have been innumerable, all to the aid of the local community, many of whom have relied upon her at one time or another.

185. Doctors and staff at Ystrad Mynach surgery where patients are advised and helped on the road to recovery whenever needed. The line-up is Dr. Greville, Dr. Thomas, Dr. Jones and Dr. Shah. The ever-helpful staff are Gwen Medal, Ann Male, Martha Davies, Jean Page, Phyllis Davies, Sue Harries, Elaine Parez, Jill Beck and Irene Gibson.

186. District Nurses Margaret Stuart and Vi Griffiths receive valuable and sometimes essential syringe drivers from Gelligaer Community Council Chairman, Graham Hughes, the costly items having been donated by the council. The nurses who are based in Oakfield Street Ystrad Mynach are very much a part of everyday life in the community and much appreciated by all who rely on their care and attention.

187. The St. John Ambulance Service is another most valuable asset for community life and Cefn Hengoed can proudly justify its enthusiasm for the organisation. Pictured here during the 1940s are the nurses who were winners of the Grand Prior Badge, the first such team in Wales. At the back are Mrs. Skinner and Mrs. Bruton (Area Officer) and in the front are Diane Thomas, Sylvia Stook, Gwyneth Williams and Ann Smith.

188. A well composed photograph of the St. John Ambulance team taken in the school grounds Cefn Hengoed, this particular team being victorious in many competitions with Superintendent David Henry Phillips at the helm and Mr. Cled Williams in the heart of it all. Seen here are - Back: George Davies, Jim Fowler, ?, Jack Kemp, A.O. Evans, Stan Cynon, Harry Smith, Bill Price and Arthur Price junior. Middle: Jimmy Kemp, Bob Williams, Dr. John Phillips, David Henry Phillips, Arthur Price senior, Jack Price and Hopkin Farr. Front: Elvet Phillips, Denzil Phillips, Cled Williams and Sam Brownett.

189. A pleasant day out for the ladies of Hengoed is photographed here in 1952 and for younger readers of this book, these were the fashions *'to be seen in'* fifty years ago. Some names have been recalled as follows - Phyllis Davies, Mrs. Coombes, Mrs. Ireland, Cissie Oliver, Bopa Whatley, Mrs. Williams, Mrs. Jones, Mrs. Webb, Mrs. Piper, Gwladys ?, Mrs. Pugh, Lizzie Herbert and Gwen Oliver.

190. A rare photograph taken in Thomas Street Maesycwmmer in 1947-48 with Val Williams in the front of the picture. Some readers may remember a very popular little corner shop at end of the cottages which was owned by Cassie Herbert (nee Roberts). Some of the other residents are Mrs. Stemp, Mrs. Hodges, William and Edith Roberts, the little boy being the son of Ted Rogers. Another building which was at the end of the row was the British Legion Club.

TABOR ROAD MAESYCWMMER Chris Griffin 77   LLANCAIACH FAWR NELSON Chris Griffin 78

TY CWRDD HENGOED , SEFYDLWYD 1650 Chris Griffin 83
HENGOED BAPTIST CHAPEL , ESTABLISHED 1650

191. The name of Chris Griffin will be well known to many, a professional artist who has displayed his talents and unorthodox techniques in various forms over the years. After leaving The Royal College of London with an MA Degree in fine arts, he became a household name in the valleys with his fine pen and ink sketches, some of which have been reproduced here and he stands alongside one of his more modern paintings *'Evening Glow'*.

192. The grounds of Ystrad Fawr were some of the finest available in the Rhymney Valley for celebrations and social events such as this combined carnival scene from the 1930s. Carnival Queen is Mary Davies (Roberts) and also in the picture are Glynis Davies, E. Jarman and David Davies.

193. June 2nd 1953 was Coronation Day for Queen Elizabeth II and Hengoed was one of the many local towns to celebrate the event with a carnival. Pictured here in Alexandra Road are Barbara Roberts as the carnival queen assisted by Joyce Ireland, Silvie Matthews, Jean Hughes and Teresa Ham.

194./195. The year 1951 was when The Festival of Britain was held to mark the centenary of the Great Exhibition of 1851 which at the time was said to have been the greatest show ever produced in the whole world! Residents of Tredomen appear in these two carnival photographs, the upper picture being the ladies football team who were due to challenge a men's side and below more impersonators have taken to a lorry. Amongst both pictures are Ivy Warren, Margaret Maryland, Florrie Phillips, Vi Donovan, Lil Bennett, Edna Smith, Ivy Anthony, Reg Donovan, Tom Bennett and Mel Baker.

196. A 1950s carnival float that is still remembered by some today as being one of the finest ever produced entitled *'The Wedding'*. The players are made up of the following - Hazel Bickham (bride), Brian Elliott (groom), Jean Lewis (bridesmaid), David Hart (vicar) with pageboy and girls Melvina Bowers, Amanda Pandy, Catherine McCarthy, Gary Jay and Ann Jay.

197. The residents of the Crescent Cefn Hengoed were well noted for their enthusiasm when it came to such things as celebrating important events, even adding colour to the kerbstones and flower pots when needed. This is a large street party held in 1951 and includes such faces as Maud Morgan, Geoff Morgan, Tony Palmer, Ann Palmer, Mrs. Williams, Alan Jay, Michael Palmer, Clive Edwards, Michael Lewis, Ron Corbin, Hazel Bickham, Jean Lewis, John Edwards, Linda Cross, Eileen Edwards and Mr. and Mrs. Cross.

198. The cottage shown in the photograph and decorated with bunting and flags for either the 1935 Silver Jubilee or 1937 Coronation, was the site of the original Lindsay Club; this building stood where the Hengoed Hall Nursing Home is now situated. An ex-Army hut was purchased and erected at the rear of the garden, it being used until new premises were built, before finally moving to the new building on today's site. Many readers will need reminding that when this photograph was taken there was no such thing as lager, and a pint of bitter was around 2p rather than today's £2!

199. Maesycwmmer School 1977. Top row: Nicola Davies, Lynette Davies, Lisa Faloon, ?, ?, Paul Davies, Phillip Cooper. Middle row: Mark Waite, Mark Holly, Jason ?, ?, Ruth Gibbon, Lindsey Jex, ?, Phillipa Walker. Bottom row: Non Evans, David Lawrence, ?, Richard Barnam, Steve Jarrett, Paul Bolton, Paul Elliot and Paul Griffin.

200. Some of the lads of Cefn Hengoed and Hengoed are caught playing a covert game of cards at the back of the Institute in the 1960s with Malcolm Boucher standing guard with a billiard cue. The card players are Roy Barry, Alun Griffiths, Tommy Pritchard, Benny Greenaway, Vivian Clapham, Michael Lewis, Graham (Noggin) Morgan, Kenny Briggs, Ronald George and Gerald Briggs.

201. Residents of Beechfield Avenue, Alexandra Road, Cefn Road and Brynavon Terrace are gathered outside the old bakehouse enjoying a 1950s celebration. A few names have come to light such as Mrs. Holder, Barry Jones, Geoff Holder, Graham Pearce, Angela Roles, Gwyn Holland, Barbara ?, Jean Roles, ? Evans, Mrs. Roles and Mrs. Norman.

202. Proving that football is not for *'men only'*, these Hengoed players are pictured in 1969 during some Investiture celebrations. Charity matches between the sexes was a popular event at the time and June Williams recalls the ladies winning the game and being presented with a *'make-do trophy'* - a chamber pot wrapped in silver foil! The team includes Sylvia Lucas, Grace Milton, Lorraine Lewis, Valerie Jones, Kath Thomas, Beverley Robinson, Gwyneth Rees, Rena Berrill, June Williams, Gwladys Powell, Ellen Price, Pamela Cooper and Stella Williams.

203. The ladies skittles section of the Non Political Club Bedwlyn Road, Ystrad Mynach was formed in 1974, playing in the Rhymney Valley League and, providing time for many a *'girls night out'* and laughs along the way. Some ladies seen here are Winnie Williams, Edna Cannon, Rosie Price, Lesley Jones, Sue Jones, Margaret Williams, June Williams, Glenys Caple, Ann Bishop, Glenys Jones, Mary Johnson and Esther Taylor.

204. Billy Bedwlyn as he was affectionately known, with a dairyman and farmer in the year 1900. This photograph which was taken outside the Beech Tree, illustrates local farming methods of a hundred years ago, a cart heavily loaded with hay (more than likely all by hand and pitchfork) and a horse that was probably well acquainted with the hill that lay in front of it.

205. A young Aubrey Haywood is being shown the skills of farming by his father Cliff in Cefn Hengoed during the 1930s. This scene in the fields of the village, portrays the hard work that latter day farmers had to contend with, and with haymaking being thirsty work, every farmhand relished the time when the ladies brought that jug of cider or water. Cliff is seen here at the age of 39, Aubrey is 11 and Jim Williams was 45 at the time.

206. Many fine outings by coach were organized by Gwynns Garage Ystrad Mynach, this particular one being to Builth Wells and the Epynt in the 1950s. Everyone enjoyed the annual motorcycle event held on Mynydd Epynt with many celebrity riders attending and some of Gwynns staff and guests are Bill Gwynn, Mr. Gwynn senior; Gwyn Jones, Dave Thomas, Arthur Evans, Bill Coles, Bill Banfield, Enid Banfield, Glyn Williams, Mr. and Mrs. Len Caple, David Bishop and Don Branwen.

207. Members of The Crosskeys Darts Team Cefn Hengoed, with a splendid array of trophies, are pictured outside the pub's jug and bottle (jug and bottle deriving from days when customers would bring their own such containers for filling with ale and stout for home consumption - an early example of a Takeaway in the town). A number of gentlemen seen here include Tom Murphy, Dai Ellis, Percy Lewis, Jackie Cullen, Mervyn Jones, Arthur Sullivan, Gordon Bishop, Ben Jones, Ken Franklin, Mrs. Williams (landlady), Frank Cochran, Edgar Phillips, Timmy Lane and Dai Ireland (Double Top).

208. This time it's the turn of the Royal Oak in Ystrad Mynach to receive an airing with this photograph of Penallta workmen's snooker team in the 1950s and in view are Eddie Lessimore, Rev Hill, David Jones, Inspector Evans, Gwylim Ivor Davies (sec.), Josh Williams (marker at the hall), Oliver Coombes, William Owen and Iestyn Owen.

209. The A.T.C. 2353 Squadron Ystrad Mynach No.2 and names to look out for are - Back: Michael Mylan, Lyndon Williams, ?, Dave Blackwell, Brian Heffron, ? Yeoman, ?, Graham Morris, Alan Thomas, ?, Lyn Baker, ?, ?, Alan Rudge, Robert Jones, ?, ?, Julian Grobski, ?, Philip Dowel, Elwyn Eddington, Dave Morgan, ?, K. O'Connell, Kerry Jones, Dave Edmunds. Front: Jeff Rodway, Jeff Matthews, F/Lt. Rudge, F/O Tommy Davies, F/O Burgin, CO RAF Turnhill, AOC Rev Davies, Dennis Summers, ? and Mel Davies.

210. Maesycwmmer has always been noted for its strong community spirit as evidenced by this carnival event staged during the Prince of Wales's Investiture in 1969. The 'star' players are Barry Skelding, Janice Baker, Eileen Russell, Terry Powell and a *'real'* son in the pram aged 5 months. The other two babies are Adrian Barwood and Gouchy Evans.

211. The Boys Club Ystrad Mynach was formed in about 1933 in the Labour Party Hall at the station end of Lewis Street before moving to Moose Hall a corrugated shack in Lisburn Road. By 1936 the club was well established and new premises were opened where the building stands today. Some of the founders of the club were Isaac Pugh, David Jones (Snowy), Hywell Jones, Mr. Jonathan, Tom Brooks and Mr. Davies the bank. The photograph above was taken during a visit by the late Duke of Gloucester (centre) with Hywell Jones and Isaac Pugh.

212. Boys Club of Wales Champions 1959 and that is what is being celebrated in this photograph with this Ystrad Mynach team of under 18s who were the first to win the championship, beating Treharris in the final. Back Row: Isaac Pugh, Joe Brownsword, Mrs. Brownsword, Clive Jones (Trainer), David Hughes, Jacky Griffiths, ? Griffiths, Geoff ?, Hywell Jones, Ron Walters, George Jonathan (Boys Club President). Front: Lionel Saunders, Frankie Gater, Len Huzzey, Roy Cross (Captain), David Arthur, Winston Dainton and Billy Chandler.

213. In 1986 Mrs. Harman of Hengoed who at the time was 67 years of age, was one of the first female club leaders to be awarded the Silver Dagger for best club leader in Wales, a competition sponsored by the Wilkinson Sword Company. The Golden Jubilee was celebrated in 1986 and the club was honoured with a visit by the Duke of Gloucester (president of the National Association of Boys Clubs), who congratulated Mrs. Harman on her twenty years as club leader. Also in the pictuire are Dave Harman and Billy Norman.

214. The Boys and Girls Club during a visit to Bolton, the leader being Ken Pritchard assisted by Tony Honeywill, Tanner Davies and Tom Pritchard. Also in the picture are Sylvia Pritchard, Robert Andrew, Shaun Loxton, Dai Pritchard, Rees Price, Jonathan Blewitt, James Powell, Kenneth Pritchard, Sarah Rowlings, Kirsty Thomas, Catrin Saunders, Ann Marie Thomas, Rhian Price, Rhian Woods, Kimberly Vale, Joanne Powell, Christopher Brideaux, Shaun Powell, Steven Pritchard, Geraint Thomas, Daniel Jones, Michael George, Clare Mackenzie, Samantha Davies, Leanne Bruford, Mark Williams, Victoria Butts, Lisa Butts and Clare MacDonald.

Acknowledgements

The authors wish to express their sincere thanks to the undermentioned who kindly loaned photographs and information used in the compilation of this book.

Jennifer Amor, Gladys Andrews, Joyce and Bill Arnott, Staff at Ashburne Print and Copy, Edna and Roy Barry, Mrs. Basso, Peter Bennett (Industrial and Maritime Museum), Ray Bishop, Mrs Boardman, Linda Boardman, Joy Bowen, Cassie Bowers, Luigi and Elvira Bracchi, Mervyn Burch, Clare Cannon, Sylvia Carroll, Cefn Hengoed OAP Association, Pat Chidgey, Graham Court O.B.E., Sian Cribb, Phyllis Davies, Jean and Leonard Davies, Mary Davies, Audrey and Vi Davies, Father Malcolm Davies, Hywell Davies (Book on Holy Trinity), Mel and Pat Davies Philip and Gail Dowell, John and Janice Drayton, Staff at Edwardian Studio, Margaret Ellis Norman Evans, Mr. and Mrs. Roy Evans, Lynne Everson, Trevor Everson, John Farmer, Jane Fennell, Bob Fordham, Walter Frame, Dai Gardiner, Val Gittins, Chris Griffin, Gillian Griffiths Kenny Harrison, Alan and Jane Hayter, Paul Hayter, Tommy Haywood, Brian Heffron, Laura Hilton, Brenda Hobbs, Lyn and Ted Hobbs, Terry Hockey, Peggy Holder, Gwladys Holder, Geof Holder, Stuart Holloway, Anne Holmes, Susan Holton, Tony Honeywill, Janet and Gareth Hopkins, Jack Hopkins, Jean and Cliff Horrell, Paul James, Connie Jenkins, Bonita Jenkins Byron Jones, Eileen Jones, George and Elaine Jones, Graham Jones, Graham and Marion Jones Gwyn Jones, Lisa Jones (Ystrad Mynach Library), Miss Nesta Jones, Olwen Jones, R.W. (Bob) Jones, Whitney Jones (Book on Maesycwmmer), Mr. Keen, Betty Kendall, Colin Kirkham, Ray Lawrence, Jane Lee, Philip Lee, Janet Lester, Glyn and Brenda Lucas, John McDonald, Marge Mallon, William and Eira Mallon, Lena Massari, David Matthews, Ellien Meara, Mrs. Mills and family, Alan Morgan, Chris Morgan (Tredomen Tourist Office), Elaine Morgan, Wendy Morgan Eric Mountford, National Museum of Welsh Life, Dr. Sue Noake and photographer, Linda Osborne, Derek Packer, Hilary Phillips, Linda Pope, Susan Price, Tommy Price, Ken Pritchard Tom Pritchard, Margaret Decima Pugh (Llewellyn), June Rao, Betty Rees, Evan Richards, Susan Richards, Barbara and Arthur Roberts, Mary Roberts, Ann Rogers, Allan and Cridwen Rogers Glenys Seaward, Dino Spinetti, John Sidoli, Rina Sidoli, Desi Smith, Mrs. Steiner, Sylvia Stook Beryl Taylor, Billy Thomas, Ceri Thomas, Dave, Pat, Gareth and Gillian Thomas, Dorothy Thomas, Gary Thomas, Gethyn Thomas, Mike Thomas, Paul Turner, Colin Walters, Sally Watkins, Alan Webb, John West, Steve Whittle, Dilla Wilkinson, Brian and Megan Wilkins, June Williams (nee), Marilyn Williams, Val Williams,